Between the
SHEETS

Between the SHEETS

A SURVIVAL GUIDE TO SAILING

BARRY WATERS & JAMES POND
ILLUSTRATED BY GRAHAM THOMPSON

'And sometimes sent my ships in fleets,
All up and down among the sheets.'

Robert Louis Stevenson, 'The Land of Counterpane'

SPHERE BOOKS LIMITED

SPHERE BOOKS LTD

Published by the Penguin Group
27 Wrights Lane, London W8 5TZ, England
Viking Penguin Inc., 40 West 23rd Street, New York, New York 10010, USA
Penguin Books Australia Ltd, Ringwood, Victoria, Australia
Penguin Books Canada Ltd, 2801 John Street, Markham, Ontario, Canada L3R 1B4
Penguin Books (NZ) Ltd, 182–190 Wairau Road, Auckland 10, New Zealand

Penguin Books Ltd, Registered Offices: Harmondsworth, Middlesex, England

First published in Great Britain by Pelham Books Ltd 1987
Published by Sphere Books Ltd 1988

Made and printed in Great Britain by
Richard Clay Ltd, Bungay, Suffolk

Contents

For Annika and Nicholas

With thanks to those other Survival Sailors:
T.D.; B.T.L.; P.M.K.; J.C.; M.J.; J.S.; C.N.
– and R.B. down under!

Introduction

"And Noah he often said to his wife when he sat down to dine,
'I don't care where the water goes if it doesn't get into the wine.'"

G. K. Chesterton, 'Wine and Water'

It wasn't that long ago that sailing really did mean '*messing* about in boats'. Climbing under a dripping hull in February and tarring yourself and your craft with some evil brew of anti-fouling was a mucky old business. 'Pushing the boat out' meant water breaking over the top of your hip boots every bit as much as it meant breaking open a bottle or three in the cockpit. No wonder they used to say that only the fool of the family went to sea. Who else would have wanted to?

But the arrival of those walk on/walk off boats, with their gleaming 'easy-care' glassfibre hulls, all high-gloss and hi-tech (and high prices), has changed all that. The number of 'fools' afloat can now be counted in millions. And those individuals who used to find the 'irresistible lure of the sea' perfectly resistible are pretty much of a minority these days.

No sooner have most of us stopped playing with toy boats in the bath than we're out there playing around in the bigger bath of the marina. It's never too late, it seems, to have a happy childhood. There we all are 'getting away from it all' in one of those nautical parking lots that keep on sprouting up around our coasts. So much so, that on a bank holiday the tail-backs on our motorways are as nothing to the log-jam of boats battling for a bit of sea-room on our waterways.

It's not an easy phenomenon to explain. Is it simply the appeal of all that snazzy sailing gear? The thrill of nosing ahead of the next boat? Or perhaps it's true, as they say, that the sea is in our blood – as well as, all too frequently, inside our yellow wellies and seeping down under our oilies. (Some things never change.) 'Water, water everywhere,' as the Ancient Mariner so rightly said. Life itself, of course, emerged from the primeval ooze; and the human body is still at least two-thirds water.

Maybe that's the reason for this obscure urge we all seem to feel to get out on the briny – the wind in our hair, the spray on our face, the exhilaration of 'racing' along at 5 mph (even the America's Cup must be about the most expensive way of travelling rather slowly), with wet Marlow chafing our hands and plenty of invigorating exercise for our cramped stomach muscles as we set to work on the bilge pump.

Ah, for the life afloat! Wine cooling in the loo-pan, Force 10 on the horizon, your last change of underwear swinging in the galley and yet another delicious meal of hot tomato soup coming to the boil (slowly). Then, when the day is done, there's the pleasure of being lulled to sleep by the gentle slosh of water in the bilges, the refrain of canned music carrying across the drink, the jangling of slatting halyards against a thousand alloy spars, to be awakened the next morning by the roar of outboard motors, as you prepare to face the exciting challenges of the day ahead – the queue for the loos, and doing battle with the harbour master.

Now, it may just be that you are one of those who feel that there are better ways of shaking up the wine. You may suspect that there's a rather good reason why 'the senior service' can't wait to step ashore when they dock. And what about all those newspaper headlines about offshore races 'ending in tragedy'?

Be that as it may, these days, it seems, all of us 'must go down to the seas again' (and again). There's just no escape. What with our maritime heritage; and what with nowhere in the country being more than 100 miles from the coast, the fact is that *no True Brit can afford not to have done a spot of sailing.*

And that's where this book comes in. Today's sailing scene has become so complex that you almost need to go on a special course just to learn to do up all the fastenings on your natty ocean-racing jacket. It can take quite a while to get to know your way around. This guide to 'Survival Sailing' aims to show you a few short cuts – or, at least, to provide you with more help than you'll get from your fellow *matelots.* After all, one of the greatest pleasures of the sport is still watching other sailors cock it up.

Of course, you can choose to learn the hard way. As the old salts will tell you, 'the only way to learn to sail is to sail'. But what with the price of boats, not to mention all the ancillary gear and clobber, this can come expensive. And anyway sailing is no longer just about sailing. These days après sail is probably bigger than sail; walking the dock as vital a skill as walking the deck. Getting it right onshore is every bit as important as getting it right offshore. For one thing, there will be a damn sight more people watching. (If the statistics are anything to go by, very few marina-berthed boats ever actually put out to sea.)

With this book, though, you should be on course right from the start. You may not be much of a sailor, but there's no reason why you shouldn't *look* like one. So, even if your love of the sea is only oil-skin deep, not to worry. Once you've mastered the skills of survival sailing (which the old salts have always kept very much to themselves), you should be a match for anyone at the yacht club bar – if not fleets ahead of them. You'll probably even be able to take on the sort of Barnacle Bill who can tie a triple bowline behind his back. (Fortunately, though, there aren't too many of this sort left any more – as we've indicated, a new breed of 'Marina Mariner' has begun to take over the sport.)

Many of the basics are really quite easy to grasp – like learning in which direction to throw your paper plates so that they don't blow back on board; the importance of chundering *with* the wind rather than into it; how to tack off suddenly to avoid an overloaded trolley careering towards you down a marina ramp. In no time at all, you too will have learnt how to weigh down your bottles and crumple your beer cans – carpeting the ocean floor for all the world like an experienced yachtmaster.

We won't be wasting too much time, however, on showing you how to cope with the Bigger Challenges of the deep. There doesn't seem to be all that much point now that most of the Great Passages have been made. After all, the long solo sail has become almost commonplace nowadays. If you are that way inclined, though, there's still the chance to make the first *genuine* single-handed round-the-world voyage, i.e. doing it with one hand tied behind your back (and no cheating).

True, there are some who would argue that sailing one of the world's Big Ponds is still The Greatest Test. It's wet out there; and cold; and deep; and dark. Just you against the elements – and any sharks, sea-snakes or killer whales that happen to be passing.

But the Survival Sailor will probably find quite enough challenges close to shore – on the low seas rather than the high seas (not *too* low, of course, if you're mooring on top of the posts on an ebb tide). The Open Sea may be a cruel mistress; but so too, you will find, is the harbour master, who will also extract his dues. The sea and the wind may be free (for the moment anyway) – but your mooring won't be. Make no mistake, you can have a very tough weekend at the marina without even putting out to sea – vacuuming and swabbing away on your floating caravan.

Another good reason for staying by the shore, of course, is the legendary camaraderie of your fellow yachtsmen – until you ram their boat, or stumble down their forehatch on the way back from the pub, or forget to untie the mooring line you attached to their stanchions as you motor away. But these accidents (or 'bad handling' as they're known when *you*'re the injured party) will happen – both on shore and at sea. Careful study of this book, though, should ensure that *you* don't come off the worst.

So don't worry if you're the type who can't tie a figure-of-eight in the end of a jib sheet; or whose inclination is to sever difficult knots with a knife; if your 'accidental gybe' is better than your 'controlled gybe'; if you're the sort who would rather sail with his fenders down; if you still aren't sure of the difference between close-hauled and keel-hauled; or between the Admiral's Cup and the America's Cup.

Rest assured: *You're not the only one.* (As you might expect, when the only qualification for owning a boat is not seamanship but enough money in the bank.)

Once you've got the hang of Survival Sailing, though, it'll soon feel as if you've been an 'old hand' forever – perhaps not quite a master mariner but a bit of a master down at the marina. (Or, indeed, a bit of a *mistress* down at the marina – Survival Sailors, of course, can be of either sex – though for convenience we will tend to use the masculine pronoun in this book.) And with your reputation made, you'll be able to stop all that unseemly scrambling about under the foresails and spend rather more of your time with your feet under the yacht club bar rather than tucked under the toe-straps. In short, you'll be home and dry. And that, of course, is where most sailors – survival or otherwise – prefer to be.

○ WIND

Whether it's a gale or a breeze depends on whether you were out in it or not

There's always either not enough wind or too much wind

The wind is never there when you need it

It's easier to sail where the wind wants you to go than where you want to go

The wind will be ideal for sailing when you're at the office

There's always more wind at the bar afterwards than there was on the water – a Force 4 at sea is a Force 8 at the bar

1 Kitting Out

'I never understood guys who get all dressed up to sweat'

Mickey Spillane's *Mike Hammer*

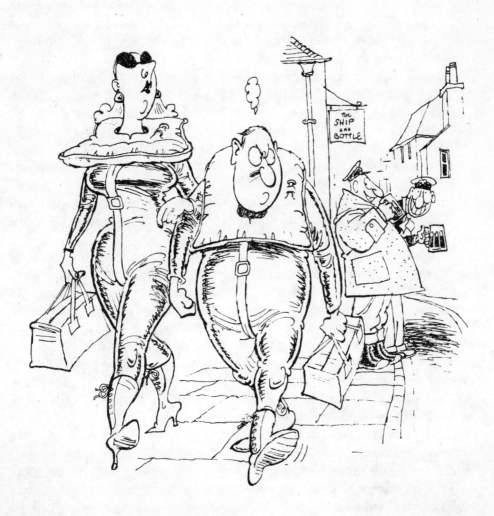

The main pre-season concern of sailors *used* to be about 'fitting out'. These days, however, it's more about 'kitting out' – all year round.

It's important that the Survival Sailor grasps this 'sea-change' from the outset. Sailing now has turned into a high-fashion 'designer' sport, sponsored by the likes of Champagne Mumm, Louis Vuitton and Rolex. And whereas you may just about get away with the occasional no-no at sea (by following the advice in this book), you can't afford any gear failures on dry land. The smallest sartorial slip-up could prove fatal to your Survival Sailing career, (for example wearing one of those blue yachting caps *with a white top*).

So, first things first. The water can wait. In fact, if you manage to develop a very strong onshore performance, it may even be able to wait forever. You'll be able to join that very select group of Survival Sailors who manage to avoid ever putting to sea at all.

You'll find you won't have missed much. The fact is that most of the action now takes place onshore. Some might even say that the object of a weekend's 'sailing' is to drive through the night, and fix yourself up in thousands of pounds' worth of equipment, simply to stand around on a dock and get drunk. 'Standing by' is what it's all about all right.

The Survival Sailor should be under no illusion, however, about the sort of investment that'll be required to cut a dash onshore. You may think there's an awful lot of money floating about on the water, but that's nothing to what people are spending on all that 'sport-tech' gear they are displaying at the water's edge.

One problem is the sheer speed with which styles change, whether it be equipment or clothing. One year it's the 'American look' (Bermuda shorts, Hawaian shirts etc). Then, before you know it, the 'New Zealand look' is in (the white shorts and rugby shirts of the offshore racing crews).

The one compensation is that you will be able to cut right back on your conventional wardrobe. It's now perfectly acceptable to use your sailing gear for everyday wear. Indeed, the Survival Sailor should make a point of being nautically togged up on almost all occasions — whether out shopping or at the office. Thus, if you fail to make your mark as the Francis Chichester of your neck of the woods, it won't be for want of trying.

You will, however, have to be prepared for a bit of competition — even from confirmed landlubbers. Sailing styles have begun to make a big impact inland. Take those tassel loafers and 'preppy' moccasins we're all wearing, which are basically cheap imitations of the original 'handcrafted' docksides (at £60 a time). And when it comes to the top-of-the-range trainers, the new hi-tech deck shoes ('transmitting moisture away from the feet', would you believe) are giving the up-market jogging shoes more than a run for their money.

Some Survival Sailors do try to give themselves the edge by wearing the sort of colours that shout louder. But even here, you won't be on your own. Everyone seems to be showing their colours these days. Remember when *all* wetsuits were black with yellow tape – compared with today's ubiquitous 'hot' or pastel shades?

And while black wellies or green wellies have served generations of Brits for shovelling snow, washing the car and walks in the country, the yellow welly is mounting quite a challenge (with the shiny red/blue offshore wellies not far behind). You might even say that whereas sailing used to be about boats, it's now a matter of boots (with inner boots, leather linings and thermal inserts, not to mention those electrical welly-warmers to slip into your boots overnight). So much for the 'Plimsoll' line.

Whoever would have thought that so much polyester and PVC ('especially designed' for sailing and with a price tag to match) could successfully challenge the established couturiers; or that Henri Lloyd would become as well known as Mary Quant used to be. Of course, Dior and Courrèges are not completely out of the picture; they still tend to determine what you wear after you change out of your racing gear to sit on the afterdeck sipping your Martini watching the sun slowly sinking below the yardarm. When it comes to something really slinky though, it's those body-hugging 'smoothskin' suits which best reveal those parts that the other sex would most like to reach out and touch. (A word of warning, though, to the not-so-trim Survival Sailor: do try to be honest with yourself before wearing one of these – they won't hold *everything* in place.)

Sailing gear, however, is not just for showing off in. It's not for nothing that the sales line is 'fashionable and *functional*'. And the Survival Sailor undoubtedly will find that it does have its uses onshore. Those heavy-weather jackets, for instance, with their built-in harnesses, are ideal for clipping your offspring to the railings in the high street while you go into Sainsbury's to do the shopping. And in these do-it-yourself days, those waist-high or chest-high sailing dungarees, which are proof against boiling fat from a gimballing cooker, are just the thing when the lady of the house sets to work with a blow-torch.

You need to be a bit careful, though, with some items. You may cut quite a dash in your ocean-racer jacket with 'hand-warmer' pockets, storm-flap and double-gusset cuffs; but, if you're in a crowded elevator and someone accidentally pulls the toggle on your built-in inflatable life-jacket, you could find yourself crushing your fellow travellers half-to-death as you expand to twice your normal size. Be careful, too, if you wear one of those 'weight' jackets designed for dinghy men (which soak up water giving you more weight to balance the boat). You can find yourself putting on five kilos in a matter of seconds if you get caught in the rain.

Sailing gear has come a long way. At one time sailors were presumed *not* to understand very much about clothes. Traditionally they used to just roll up their clobber on board. And can you think of anything more absurd than bell-bottoms for wearing on a boat? Now, of course, it's zip-up triple-lined reinforced seamless everything with velcro fastners and double rubber wrist seals and a *unique* ventilation system. (Not, it should be said, that this actually stops the water from getting into your wellies and settling around your crotch; or that it does much for the 'pong-factor' — wetsuits still smell as bad as they always did.)

The sailing style used to be 'the scruffy look'. Dinghy sailors wore army surplus khaki shorts and a pair of battered tennis shoes. For the keelboat

man, it was canvas slip-ons (with the heels trodden into the sole), an old pair of rolled up trousers and a well-patched oily wool sweater – frayed about the cuffs and never washed 'to preserve the oil'. Madame, if she was lucky, had a Guernsey, which would last the whole of her sailing career. And when the going got rough, you put on your leaky yellow oilies and stuffed a towel around your neck. No such thing as a specially designed 'neck-towel', with a little anchor or a monogram in the corner.

If sailors cut a dash at all, apart from the white flannels and blazers of Cowes Week, it was in the matter of headgear – the jaunty short-peaked yachting cap. Now, of course, you have to have a whole range of hats – woolly ones, close-fitting denim caps, balaclavas, wetsuit helmets, printed caps, not to mention those knitted headbands. (Incidentally, the Survival Sailor should avoid those caps which make you look like a chauffeur or the ones with 'skipper' emblazoned on the front – they will only serve to *undermine* your authority.)

Multiply this sort of outlay a few times for a family of five and you can see why refitting the boat is out of the question. Those kids are probably walking around wearing more than the cost of the boat itself – when you take all the accessories into account: the Bucci sunglasses; the nylon safety harness with light and whistle; the plastic floating buoy key-rings; the 'non-sinkable' waterproof sailing binoculars; the 'warm packs' to put inside your gloves, boots or down the back of your jumper; the acupuncture seasickness pressure bracelet; the titanium *chronograph* (no self-respecting sailor wears a *watch* these days – unless it happens to be a 'compass-watch' or a racing stopwatch).

And everything, of course, has to match – sweaters embroidered with the name of your yacht (or even signalling the name of your yacht in little flags), team outfits, matching headscarves, and so on. And any change of boat or sails naturally means a complete new wardrobe.

So much for 'protective' clothing – unless what is meant is 'image-protection'. Some Survival Sailors, though, may find that their image is just as well protected, and at rather less expense, by dressing 'the old way'. And it certainly need not do your reputation any harm if you stick to your salt-encrusted docksides, with the uppers coming away from the soles, and *worn without socks*.

In fact, if you do opt to dress the old way, by carefully selecting your kit you may find yourself even *adding* to your reputation. Try wearing one of those Kinsale fishermen's 'smocks' in well-worn canvas (though these nifty unisex wraparounds do seem to be threatening to come *into* fashion); and underneath, how about a fly-fronted grandpappy 'Yukon' vest? Both are garments that have stood the test of time. But they also make for the unusual sort of combination that should ensure the Survival Sailor is not lightly dismissed as just any old member of 'the old school'.

Of course, 'dressing down' may mean going to a bit of trouble – boiling up your red trousers in the washing machine for a couple of weeks till they've faded to that classic rusty shade; and trailing your deck shoes in the water behind the boat for a day or two to give them the right effect. (You'll find this easier, by the way, if you *don't* use the kind 'specially treated to repel salt water, with rot-proof thread and non-corrosive eyelets'.) However, your efforts may well be rewarded. Not only will you save yourself a few bob, but also with any luck, that salt water on your shoes may even be taken as an indication of salt water in your veins.

○ GEAR

There will be more gear on board than there are people who know how to operate it

The amount of equipment on board will exceed the amount of storage space available

The gear you brought with you will not be the gear you need

The more time you spend selecting your gear before the trip, the less useful it will be

The most necessary equipment will have been so carefully stored that no one can find it

You may have the equipment but you won't have the tools

There will be less equipment on board at the end of the voyage than there was at the start

You won't tell this to the charterer

2 Choosing your Boat

'The model you own is the only one they ever had that trouble with'

Andrew A. Rooney, *And More*

Having invested heavily in gear, the question you must now ask yourself is whether you really need (and can afford) a boat to go with it. After all, those 'real' sailors – the types who are always delivering boats – and never actually own their own; they just sail other people's. And many a Survival Sailor has concluded that there's not much point in wrecking your own boat if you can wreck someone else's.

However, if you are determined to invest in a boat, you should think very carefully about what it is you are trying to tell the world. As the Americans say, your boat is a 'lifestyle statement'. Or, to put it another way, your boat is *you* – whether you trailer-sail, or prefer to haul a longer keel.

The problem is that for most of us, our choice tends to be dictated by circumstances. And most boat-owning careers follow an all-too-familiar pattern. You start on a youngster's puddle-hopper, and progress through a range of dinghies before moving on to something larger – with berths, cooker and a loo – so that you can drag the family along. Until, that is, they get fed up with it. At which point you may well revert to a smaller craft – despite the old adage about a foot of waterline for every year of a man's age.

One thing is certain. At any given time, the boat most people dream about is *not* the one they actually sail. This is what's known as the 'escalator principle' of boat ownership: as soon as you've got a boat, you'll want a different one. Thus, your Mirror Dinghy may have seemed like the ultimate in wish-fulfilment in its day (and yours); but sooner or later (probably sooner) you'll start to feel that your wishes would be more fulfilled if your Mirror Dinghy was trailing at the end of a painter behind your computer-guided yacht, complete with bathing ladder dangling over the transom to help the bikinied lovelies clamber aboard.

This brings us, once again, to the money factor – though this is a matter that can all too easily be overlooked when it comes to boats. The man who has just told his galley-bound wife that there's no way they can afford a microwave will think nothing of popping into the chandler's shop and lashing out a hundred quid for some thoroughly dispensable nautical gizmo. Even a stainless-steel shackle can cost about as much as a piece of jewellery. (This is one of the reasons, incidentally, why chandler's shops have now begun to stock all kinds of expensive *non*-nautical gizmos – so that the wife can pop in there and take her revenge.)

The fact is, though, that boat salesmen, particularly at the Boat Show, tend to be extremely good at persuading you that money is no object. What the salesman omits to tell you, of course, is that buying your boat is one thing, but that equipping her to sail will cost you half as much again, quite apart from mooring fees and keeping her up. That's probably why there are so many rotting hulls moored around our coasts, and why the Survival Sailor can often do very well for himself by wandering around the yacht club pontoons and making a few offers: many a bankrupt Boat Show buyer will leap at the chance of getting his vessel off his hands. Ever noticed how there seem to be far more people *selling* boats than there are *buying* boats?

When it comes to making an offer, though, the Survival Sailor should make sure that *he* is the one who decides. Don't rely, for instance, on your nearest and dearest. In cahoots with the seller, they are quite capable of persuading you to get the kind of boat that would ruin your reputation for good. They can even make you momentarily forget that you're a *sailor*, and persuade you that you'd be a lot happier with a twin-screw sedan cruiser – one of those floating piano-bars with a 'lounge' or a 'saloon' rather than a cabin, complete with flying bridge and topped up with as many tiers as a wedding cake – so that the whole thing is about as tall as it is long (and about as unstable).

It's at these moments that the Survival Sailor can't afford to forget ('afford' being the operative word) that what he needs is a 'fine keel', not 'interior space' – tempted as his family may be by all that chrome, and the thick pile carpet and the en suite showers and loos. Though it may be handy for some people to have a stern that you could park the car on or accommodate a small tennis court – *the Survival Sailor is definitely not one of them.* He doesn't drive boats. He *sails* them. The Richard Bransons of this world may enjoy charging about in a sort of motorized shoe-box – but the Survival Sailor *doesn't.*

And even though you now find yacht clubs with a fair sprinkling of members who own these sorts of craft, the Survival Sailor needn't be shy about voicing his contempt. 'The bigger the boat, the bigger the amateur.' That's his view. It's what a boat can do under sail that counts: 'Used to have a twenty-two-foot Kestrel, all wood, and could she sail. Had to cook lying down, mind you. And you were always on your knees in the cabin. But that was a real boat for you.'

Not that your immediate family will necessarily agree with this. They may still feel there's something to be said for the kind of vessel that's more suited to a candle-lit dinner for four than to a cup-a-soup and a cheese sandwich, or to a pie and a pint in the pub (with your trailer-sailer in the car park outside). In short, they want a boat that will impress the neighbours. This, however, is almost bound to be a losing game. You invariably find that the person you're moored alongside has a Swan to your Westerly or a Flying Dutchman to your GP14. And anyway, most of the standard names rarely get a second glance these days.

If you *really* want to get attention without going to too much expense, the Survival Sailor will do a damn sight better to invest in a rust-caked oyster-smack or a barnacle-encrusted mussel dredger – converted for sail, of course. Not only will this discourage others from mooring alongside you, but you will also get a lot more interested and admiring glances than you would with a state-of-the-art super-sloop. And you'll also consolidate your reputation as a bit of an old sea-dog – or at least as someone who *cares* about our maritime heritage.

Then, when you want to do some real sailing, you're free to pick and choose – just the sort of flexibility the Survival Sailor needs. And if you'd rather not sail, they'll all understand when you say you've got far too much work to do on the dredger. No more anxiety either about getting branded as a Hurley man, or of feeling inferior when you pull up alongside a vintage Nicholson, or don't manage to sail your 'plastic fantastic' quite like those Kiwis in 'Freo'.

You'll sleep more soundly, too – dreaming about *sailing* and not about your boat. And on those dark and stormy nights when the tiles are blowing off your roof, you can rest easy, with none of those worries about whether your halyards are still attached to the mast, or if there's still a mast for them to be attached to.

○ BUYING AND SELLING

The boat you have is not the boat you want

The fact that you can afford the boat doesn't necessarily mean you can afford to sail it

There are more people selling boats than there are buying boats

All boats that are being advertised have something wrong with them

All boats have something wrong with them

What's not included in the price is more relevant than what is included in the price

If you have more than one child and only one dinghy, you will either have to:

          a) buy another dinghy
          b) get rid of the dinghy
          c) get rid of the extra child

3 Sailing Styles

**'We were sitting in the bow of the yacht. I'm an old
navy man; the bow is the rear end, isn't it?'**

Richard Nixon, interviewed by David Frost

Perhaps, though, we are getting ahead of ourselves. The Survival Sailor can't very well choose his boat until he's made up his mind about the sort of sailing he intends to go in for. In fact, coastal cruising will probably turn out to suit his style best. But it is, of course, only one of a number of possibilities. To help you make up your mind, therefore, here is a rundown of some of the main options. Although many of these would be better avoided, it is important that the Survival Sailor at least should be able to *talk* about them all with some authority – *as if from experience.*

○ DITCH-CRAWLING/PUDDLE-BASHING ○

At first glance, sailing on river, reservoir, lake or broad might seem ideal for the Survival Sailor. You can sail in relative safety on inland waters, thus permitting you to sail with some assurance; and there will be no shortage of pubs and cafés around the water's edge. But this impression would be a bit misleading. First of all you'll often be performing in full view of passers-by on the tow-path and of fishermen lobbing their maggots on to your deck. And those pubs are invariably situated to provide the regulars with some riverside amusement (i.e. just by that low bridge that requires you to get your mast down). It can also get a bit boring taking an eleven-foot sailing dinghy through a lock 500 times. Other problems are never knowing what's round the next bend, sudden absences of wind ('Starvation Corner'), or unpredictable fierce gusts, and all those motor cruisers which don't know the meaning of right of way, let alone 'minding their wash'.

The fact is, too, that for the up-to-date Survival Sailor, inland sailing is not really where it's at any more. It'll do your reputation no harm to reminisce about the days when you heard the bittern call on Barton Broad, but it's probably better not to go out listening all that often.

○ **WINDSURFING** ○

These are the people, you may remember, who do it standing up. The Survival Sailor, needless to say, prefers to do it sitting or lying down — as do most other sailors. Thus the windsurfer's somewhat deviant technique has led some people to question whether these upstarts on their rudderless planks actually qualify as 'sailors'. After all, they do tend to call themselves 'riders'.

But whatever they may call themselves, there's no denying that these bronzed young heretics (who tend to have an average age of fifteen and a half and lateral muscles that would catch the wind if you flexed them in the right direction) are sailors through and through. They are, in fact, probably our closest link with the origins of the sport when some caveman who lived by the river first perched himself precariously on top of a floating log and held up a pair of pterodactyl wings to try to catch the wind.

Once again, though, the Survival Sailor should be under no illusions about the sort of sums involved. There's many a sailing parent who has encouraged their offspring to take up board-sailing in the belief that this would be a *cheap* way for the youngster to learn a bit about the basic principles of wind and sail. They all too soon discover that it's not enough to have just one board. You need several, of different kinds, preferably custom-made, and constructed from hi-tech high-price materials like epoxy, polycarbonate, kevlar, carbon fibre and EPS foam, which must, of course, be airbrushed to your own personal design. (Board-sailors don't just get the old aerosol out and do their own artwork.) Then, there's the matching set of sails, with your own personal logo, and all the rest of the gear – your wetsuit, your drysuit, your smoothskin, your Bermuda clingers, your neoprene under-socks, your rubber surf shoes, your windsurf boots, your rope-soled beach-shoes, and your neoprene mittens. The thing is, though, that windsurfing gear is very much wear-and-tear gear (the battered look is very in) – so the expenditure is pretty much a constant process. Board-sailors have even begun to rival skiers as throw-away consumers.

Another thing which skiing and surfing have in common – which may be of particular relevance to the more foolhardy Survival Sailor – is that both sports are all about *keeping your balance*, which tends to mean that *lack of competence can be all too evident.* Doing it standing up is not as easy as it looks. Just try perching on one of those beach-side see-saws that novices learn on – let alone doing it in a wind and on water. And you need to be able to keep your balance not just *during*, but also *après* – when the drinking usually gets pretty heavy. Make no mistake, these youngsters would be more than a match for many of the old soaks who prop up the yacht club bar.

So a Survival Windsurfer would need to be pretty fit. You can get very stiff forearms and a very bad back from continually hauling your soaking sail out of the water for as long as you can keep clambering back on to the board for one more go. *Real* board-sailors, of course, simply 'water-start', hauling themselves up by the wishbone. These 'hot-runners' make it look very easy as they fly their board through the air off a big wave hanging there more or less upside down, yet in perfect control, as they land on top of the next wave. The chances are that your own one-handed duck gybe won't come off quite so well.

Fortunately though, for the British Survival Sailor, windsurfing is more of a sport for the sort of countries which can drum up 'frizzle' weather with some consistency. It's one thing to shoot across the limpid blue waters of the Med or the Caribbean in perfect balance with your luridly patterned fully battened 'fat-head' power sail, coming to halt with a perfect gybe, and flipping on to the golden sand. And it's quite another to do it, with no one watching, freezing to death in your rubber drysuit in the less than limpid waters of Little Puddlington Reservoir.

It's the French, in fact, who have really taken to it – 'like frogs to water'. One Air France pilot even crossed the Atlantic on one – accomplishing this insane feat in thirty-seven days, sleeping 'on board' at night in the mid-Atlantic swell, wrapped up in a sort of inflatable air mattress. Thus the British Survival Sailor needn't feel too badly about leaving board-sailing to those over-toasted Latins and a few of his nuttier countrymen. The best tack for the Survival Sailor is probably to take a slightly amused indulgent attitude to this *simple* sort of sailing, while you busy yourself with the finer points of boatmanship in all its glorious complexity. Not that it'll do your reputation any harm to have a few battered boards propped up outside the garage – mainly 'for the kids', of course, and for those one or two weekends a year when you feel like 'getting back to basics'.

○ DINGHIES ○

As far back as 1928 when Uffa Fox produced 'Avenger' the first planing version of the International 14 dinghy, dinghy sailing used to be what it was all about where thrills on the water were concerned. And although so much of the dinghy scene is part of history, dinghy sailing is something the Survival Sailor *can't afford not to have done*. Whole generations learnt to manoeuvre on water in those cheap 'marine-ply' boats (made from plywood developed from the Mosquito bomber), that followed after the war.

In the Fifties and Sixties sailing meant *dinghy* sailing. Everything else was too expensive in those pre-affluent society days before the bulge-generation grew up and found they needed a cruiser to accommodate the wife and kids. It was all Mirrors and Herons, Cadets and Enterprises, GPs and Fireflys, Merlin Rockets and National 12s – with the fashions changing from year to year, going from hyper-complicated blocks with small pulleys to single whips around giant gin blocks.

Hundreds of boats would complete in the national championships. *And the Survival Sailor could well have been one of them* – which may explain why (at the yacht club bar) he's still so obsessed with sail shape and go-fast ploys.

Today, however, the Survival Sailor may prefer to keep his bottom dry; and even if he has the stomach muscles for it, leaning out horizontally and riding a trapeze skimming the water in a ten-knot plane is one sure way of getting your pants wet. And unfortunately that tends to be what dinghy sailing is all about these days.

It's the Laser boys (and girls) who are somewhat to blame. These snappy fourteen footers, now the largest class in the world, seem to have managed to buck the trend of the great dinghy decline, creating a sort of cult for the young and strong who prefer a tiller to a sail-boarder's wishbone.

The problem with Laser-racing (and racing is what it's all about) is that it often takes place on the wilder reaches of the open sea in winds somewhat stronger than light airs. You also tend to need to be 6 feet 5 inches, tall and weigh fourteen stone in order to keep the boat vertical. Little wonder that these characters are said to be in demand as crew for America's Cup boats.

Fortunately, there are still plenty of other types of dinghy around which should suit the Survival Sailor rather better. A lot of youngsters continue to learn to sail in Cadets (when Dad is not learning at the same time that is — in which case a Mirror comes into its own). On the Continent, aspiring six-year-old Olympic helmsmen opt for the Optimist — a tiny soap-box (which is what it originally was) single-hander.

Another class found virtually everywhere is the Hobie Cat. The Survival Sailor, however, should beware though of this innocent-looking catamaran, often seen around the shores of the Med looking not unlike a pedalo with brightly coloured sails. These Californian inventions can go a bit, are very tricky to sail well and have an unfortunate habit of burying one of the hulls in a wave, catapulting inexperienced and unsuspecting crewmen huge distances over the shark-infested waters where they are often sailed.

Mind you, sailing one of these things shouldn't be beyond the veteran Survival Sailor who claims to have cut his nautical teeth on roll-tacking a Firefly or being bashed over the head with the boom while capsizing an Enterprise at the gybe mark in a Force 6. 'Those were the days,' our Survival Sailor might reminisce at the bar, recalling those glorious brass-monkey winters on the reservoir and the river, and the joys of trailing away to the almost equally chilly pleasures of the sea in summer.

That's why the Survival Sailor will often take an indulgent attitude to today's windsurfers. Remember how those Fireflies used to troop off en masse to some sedate seaside resort and turn the town upside down after spending the day being turned upside down on the water.

In fact, *many a Survival Sailor likes to hang on to (or acquire) an ancient Firefly* — just for old time's sake, and to keep alive those glorious memories of sailing her flat and fast to windward in a slight chop. If you're rash enough to take her out, though, and you try to get her up on a plane and something goes wrong, do remember that when you tell the story later you didn't 'capsize', you were 'overpowered'.

Of course, it's not just out there on the water that dinghy sailing has its hazards and inconveniences. Dinghy parks are invariably damp, muddy and crowded. And the pleasures of wading in waist-deep to get one launched are second only to hitching up the trailer in the rain at the end of an open meeting – either slipping a disc as you pull her on or backing up the car and smashing your tail lights. And don't expect any help from the fellow parked next to you – not if he sails a different kind of boat. Those 'one-design' rivalries are as fierce as ever among dinghy folk – a tradition that goes right back to the aggro between the National 12 and the (then) upstart Firefly which the Twelve sailors described as being less like a dinghy in construction and more like a 'steam pudding' (because of the way she was moulded together in an oven).

This fierce brand loyalty can actually serve the Survival Sailor rather well. 'Once a Firefly man always a Firefly man' he can tell the Laser racer defiantly, pointing proudly to that twenty-five-year-old wooden hull rotting on its cradle under a tarpaulin at the bottom of the garden. Chances are, the Laser man will understand what he means.

○ DAYSAILING ○

These open keelboats might perhaps suit the sort of Survival Sailor who has social aspirations. For it's here that you tend to find the blue bloods and Hooray Henrys (and Henriettas), roaring down to the coast on a summer weekend to race their Dragon, Flying Fifteens, Darings, Etchells, X-One Designs, and the poshest of all – the six-metres. And this type of sailing does not merely offer the advantages of style and class (kings have twice won Olympic gold medals), as well as the chance to hobnob with the right people at the club bar and dinner afterwards ('correctly dressed' of course rather than 'smart-casual'). The boats themselves have the comforting feel of a ton of lead underneath: this allows for a little heeling over but with little risk of the indignity of getting your mast stuck in the mud or of a full capsize – the trademark of the dinghy brigade with their wetsuits, life-jackets and trapeze harnesses. Little wonder that these boats are so popular with bankers and city types. Like a blue-chip company, they may alter their position from time to time, but they are rock solid down below.

All in all then, a possibility for the Survival Sailor – provided he can afford to keep up appearances (and the boat) both *on* and *off* the water, and doesn't mind being thought of as a bit of a snob – or an imposter (like those dinghy sailors in disguise – the J 24s).

○ INSHORE CRUISING ○

This is where the generation lost to dinghy sailing seems to have fetched up – and where the Survival Sailor is likely to feel most at home. There's probably a wider range of boats in this category than you used to find in dinghys in their heyday – everything from boats not much bigger than a Wayfarer dinghy with a lifting keel, a cabin on top and bucket-and-chuck-it sanitation, right up to the top-of-the-range luxury yachts with their cedar-lined lockers, integrated satellite navigation systems, and ensuite superloos.

So not only should the Survival Sailor be able to find a boat that suits his style; with a cruiser *he should have his best chance of concealing any lack of sailing skill.* Of course, the Survival Sailor may well have enjoyed going hard into the wind in his dinghy days, but now with the family aboard, it seems fairer somehow to pick a course going across or down wind. And tempted as he often is to do a little heavy weather sailing or to gybe that spinnaker, somehow he doesn't very often seem to 'get the chute out of the turtle'.

The names of the boats tend to reflect this change in sailing style: 'Gee 'n' Tee', 'Yes Dear', 'Spring Clean', 'Blue Water', 'Mon Ami' as compared with the dinghy sailor's 'Oh Oh', 'Bodily Functions', 'Gopher Broke', 'Nice Legs', 'Do You Mean Me?' (But at least both categories show a bit more imagination than the windsurfers who let the manufacturers name the boards – 'Hy-Jumper', 'Limited Edition', 'UFO'.)

The fact is that, despite a bit of a trend towards single-handed sailing, the cruising keelboat is basically about communal, if not domestic, life at sea. Not that it's without its hazards, which will be explored in more detail in later chapters. But there's no getting away from it: the social side does tend to loom large in cruising and these are the sailors who tend to be the mainstays of the yacht club bar – 'sitting it out until the weather improves'.

Of course, you do get the odd 'Joshua Slocum' (putting tintacks on the deck to discourage the natives from stepping aboard). And a lot of those signs saying 'No Mooring' or 'Reserved For' do seem distinctly unfriendly. But, for all that, there are quite a number of boats who are ready enough to hoist the gin pennant and open a couple of tins of peanuts. Not that this will always contribute to domestic harmony when the ship's mistress hears the skipper of their twenty-two foot ketch call out: 'It's all right – we can easily squeeze in another dozen.'

○ **OFFSHORE** ○

This sort of thing – either 'IOR' (International Offshore Rule) racing or Blue Water cruising – tends to be a bit outside the range of most Survival Sailors. A money-no-object world of millionaires with wet bottoms, hired skippers, professional crews and glamorous women who live in a style to which many of us would like to become accustomed. The club is the RORC; the magazine is *The Seahorse*; and the object is to *win at all costs*. As the old saying has it, 'offshore racing is just like standing under a cold shower tearing up $1000 bills'. Or, as one commentator put it, 'The mating-dance of the lead-bottomed money-gobblers.'

This is a game for the big boys – whether you're a 200 lb. winch-grinder with forearms like cured hams, or have the sort of bank account that can keep a team of winch-grinders fed on prime beef five times a day, as well as providing them with all the latest 'spar-wars' technology and the sort of boffin-designed Twelve-metre yachts on which they can display their skills. As that pre-Perth America's Cup 'Big John' song went: 'There's a man in Perth with a job to do; and all he's got is a boat and a crew – Big Bond.' The song omitted to add that 'Bondy' (and his wife 'Big Red') unlike Big John, have also got a great deal of the folding stuff.

It also helps if you can sail a bit – preferably like 'Big Bad' Dennis Conner completing 'some unfinished business' against Australia's Kookaburra III – with a little bit of help from that grooved friction-reducing plastic film on his keel and his buxom new 'Dolly Parton' spinnaker. (The US Syndicate's fight song: 'Ain't no doubt about it, we won't leave Perth without it.')

You will run into the occasional 'rorkie' (or so he claims) at the yacht club bar. But that's about as close as most of us are likely to get to the big league – although all that America's Cup razzamataz of recent years has begun to have an impact on local yacht clubs. Designers of family cruisers seem to be giving them that sleek-lined rorkie look. And club racers are also going in for their own team symbols, insignia and 'battle flags.'

It may not be too long before even the handicap racers at Little Pudlington Yacht Club are all kitted out in their matching hooped 'Canterbury-look' shirts, and getting themselves off to a flying start with one of those Maori chants that the All Blacks perform before steamrollering the British Lions. They may even find a use for their 'groovy' old gramophone records, melting them up with tin-foil to spray on the bottom of their boats. (Survival sailors incidentally should avoid trying to do this *during* the competition – unlike the Kookaburra squad who had divers over the side in the shark-infested waters spraying on their go-fast concoction minutes before the gun for the third race against Conner.)

And if you wander round Little Pudlington this winter and peek into a few back gardens, you may well see that not a few of the boats parked there under the lean-to have those curtains draped around their hulls. Clearly, Pudlington's top racers don't intend to make the same mistake that Alan Bond did after Australia II's America's Cup win in 1983, when he rashly hoisted that celebrated winged keel out of the water for all the world to see (and copy). The locals have developed almost the sort of coyness Conner displayed in keeping the wraps around Stars and Stripes' Roman-nosed keel and stubby Delta-shaped wings (compared with the Bond lookalike 'maxi-spanners' on most of the other boats). As a member of the winning American team said: 'It's kind of weird – but it kind of works.'

○ **ROUND-THE-WORLD** ○

Sailing at its most masochistic – involving spending extremely long periods at sea living in conditions that would disgrace any self-respecting shanty town. The Roaring Forties may appeal to some people – but probably not to the Survival Sailor.

○ THE REST ○

Of course, the categories covered above are by no means exhaustive. There are also catamarans (if you want to double your chances of developing a hole or a leak); trimarans (if you want to triple your chances . . .); old Gaffers; boats with windmill sails; Arab dhows; converted wherries; Edwardian steamboats; Chinese junks; trawler yachts etc. etc. The list is endless. And many of these do offer a good deal of scope for the savvy Survival Sailor – on the basis that the less other people actually understand about your boat the better. So don't be discouraged from experimenting. After all, there's no need for us all to be in the same boat. And it does mean that when you come alongside in a way that your new neighbours don't exactly appreciate, you can always claim you were simply executing the traditional 'slam-landing' of a Chinese sampan. They may not quite believe you – but they'll find it hard to contradict you.

○ YOUR COURSE

You won't always get to where you intend in the way you intend

You are more likely to be off course than on course

Your course does not necessarily bear any relationship to your intended destination

It's easier to work it out on land than it is on the boat

The most accurate way to plot your course is to do it when you've arrived

It always takes longer than you expect

You are only really sure where you are when you get there

This is better than not getting there at all

---

4 Mastering your Ship

**'I've got news for you,
I'm the captain of this ship
And you're just a member of the crew'**

Little Esther, Cupid's Boogie

For reasons that will by now be clear, the Survival Sailor will usually find himself opting for keelboat cruising. But though this is the least hazardous option, it is far from being the relaxed affair that the word 'cruising' makes it sound – and it is not entirely without risk. In the following chapters, therefore, we will look more closely at the more critical aspects of cruising in an effort to help the Survival Sailor to make the best of it – or at least to avoid the worst.

One way of minimising the dangers, of course, is to stay securely moored in the marina for most of the time. This is one reason why most cruising yachts don't actually take to sea very much – rather fortunately, as a matter of fact, with waterways as congested as they are. Can you imagine what would happen if just one quarter of the yacht club boats were to head out to sea on the same day?

Even with things as they are, collision courses are almost inevitable. (The drill on these occasions, incidentally, is to insist that you were on the boat being overtaken – even though it may not have *looked* like it – and to keep quoting some obscure rule – perhaps 101, sub-paragraph four of the revised version. This should be safe enough. There are rules for everything at sea and no one really understands them.) So don't go out of your way to encourage your fellow yachtsmen to abandon their marina berths. Communal life on board is quite bad enough, without making it any harder by having to cope with the vagaries of other people's seamanship on the open water.

Note here, incidentally, the use of the term '*other people's*' seamanship. Rule number one of Survival Sailing when you're afloat is: 'Always blame it on someone else.'

No Survival Sailor worth his salt, however, will want to spend all his time hugging the shore. So, from time to time, you will find yourself on a boat clearing the harbour wall (with a bit of luck) and laying a course.

Where you go from there is anybody's guess. ('Laying a course' is generally completely irrelevant to the final destination.) But, as far as the Survival Sailor is concerned, usually the best course is to take the bull by the horns and to assume command of the vessel. This won't always be easy. The owner of the boat may rather resent someone else taking charge. But if the Survival Sailor sticks to his guns, and makes a passing reference to his yachtmaster certificate, he should find himself at the helm as 'Survival Skipper'. More often than not who controls the ship is determined less by competence than by sheer force of personality.

There are certain distinct advantages for the Survival Sailor in playing 'the great helmsman'. Being skipper, in effect, means power without responsibility. You can get everyone else to do the work – at your direction. Then, when things go wrong – as they inevitably will – you can blame it all on them.

In a family situation, this role tends to fall most easily to 'Dad', with the wife as 'galley slave' and the children as crew. The female Survival Sailor, however, need not necessarily accept any sort of subordinate position. Even when racing you do find girls who very effectively take charge at the helm – yelling at the men 'faster on that genoa winch please' and so on. It pays, therefore, for the Survival Sailor to choose his fellow rovers very carefully. Thus, getting together a scratch crew at short notice is not recommended – there's always the odd chance that one of them may know something about it.

Hence the popularity of the family situation. Here, at least, you know who you are dealing with. But the fact is that family familiarity can breed a degree of contempt. So the Survival Skipper should make a point of asserting his authority right from the start and make it clear that he'll be standing no nonsense.

Of course, you shouldn't overdo the 'Captain Ahabs' and get too carried away – clapping children into leg irons at the drop of a shackle pin, or having them continually swab the decks. But do keep a firm grip, and, above all, *keep them busy*. That way they may not notice that you don't actually have a very clear idea of what you're doing for most of the time.

'A busy ship is a happy ship' – that's the Survival Skipper's motto. Plenty of sail changes – from genoa to jib and back again, and again. And don't make it too easy for them. Conceal the pliers and the hammer beforehand so that it takes a while to get the shackle undone or the sail down the luff-groove, while you keep screaming at them: 'Come on, get that sail down', 'Ease off the reef pennants, for God's sake'.

Make a point, too, of sailing hard into the wind. Don't just settle down and go in the easy directions – across or downwind. Thus you will almost constantly have about five people gathered round the mast doing battle with a viciously flailing mainsail, while you bellow: 'Come on now. Go for it. All the way. Can't you see, I'm luffing to make it come in easily.'

After a while they may get the hang of it. But don't let them become cocky. If necessary, get them to gybe the spinnaker. That should keep them tangled up for a bit, as you call out to them contemptuously that on the America's Cup boats they have ten spinnakers – 'and I have to have a crew that can't even handle one'. Incidentally, flying the kite is better performed on *someone else's* boat as spinnakers can come a bit expensive.

No sooner will this manoeuvre have been completed than you'll be at them to trim the sails properly: 'Pull, for Christ's sake. Two more turns round the winch. Put some effort into it.' And just as they think it's plain sailing: 'Come on now. Ready to tack again? Look lively. Ready about . . .'

Of course, the Survival Skipper should also show his human side – going below to make the ship's company a well-earned mug of tea (while he has a tot of brandy). *But do pick your moment carefully* – ideally when you can see trouble brewing, thus absolving yourself of any blame for the ensuing cock-up.

'Like to take her for a bit?' you ask paternally, with a squeeze on the shoulder of the least competent member of the crew, and then disappear into the well, only to be heard screaming a minute or so later as you appear in the companionway: 'You're not steering a straight course. Hold her steady. Look, we're luffing up again. Can't you see your sails are flapping? For God's sake, she's heading up into the wind.'

However, do try to be fair at all times. This means not neglecting the women on board. There's no reason why the galley should be a sort of no-go area where the women are confined. So think twice before you tell the lady to go below and to 'belt up' (to the galley, of course). After all, getting a mainsail up is a bit like fitting curtain hooks into a rail. There's no reason why the girls shouldn't do it, just as there's no reason why a woman shouldn't make an equally effective Survival Skipper.

Incidentally, if she does get the wrong point of the sail up first, take your time before saying so. Let them find out the hard way. Same thing when they put the genoa up inside the baby stay. And don't feel too badly about giving them a hard time up front on the foredeck. They have to learn some day.

No, the Survival Skipper (male or female) is not a sexist. He doesn't discriminate against the women. There's no reason, why the girls shouldn't

also enjoy the fun and have the chance to get salt water in their hair. So don't get upset when she uses your chart as a tablecloth or puts diesel in the port tank and water in the starboard. *Everyone* should have a chance to do all the different jobs. So when you draw up your toilet-cleaning rota, it should include the *whole crew* (except yourself, of course).

The Survival Skipper's concern for his crew, however, does often mean having to be cruel to be kind. Thus when someone is below deck seasick, you yell out: 'Get him/her up here.' Not only will the fresh air do them good; it may also provide the rest of the crew with a good opportunity for some 'Man Overboard' practice. (Being seasick and peeing over the side are the two most common causes of this phenomenon.)

All in all, then, the most vital quality of a Survival Skipper is confidence. So, even if you gybe all standing by mistake, and the boom slams across nearly breaking the mast, keep your nerve. Call out merrily: 'I'll make it a real Chinese gybe next time – that'll keep you on your toes.'

Admittedly, some of this advice may seem a bit harsh. It may even be one of the reasons why it's so hard to drum up a crew these days, and why the Survival Skipper so often has to rely on his own family when taking the boat out. But you should at least earn the respect of your nearest and dearest – and, in all probability, ensure that you don't have to take the boat out *too* often.

○ SEASICKNESS

The only day you forget your pills is the day you need them

The number of people who will admit to being seasick afterwards is considerably smaller than the number of people who actually were

When it first comes on, you're afraid you will die

Later you're afraid that you won't

At lunch, if you don't heave to, you may well heave up

A seasick person does not easily differentiate between windward and leeward

Despite what they say, you never do feel better up on deck

5 Close Encounters

'Both parties should keep in the best humour possible'

The Art and Practice of English Boxing, 1807

Surprisingly enough, the main problems you are likely to face as a Survival Skipper normally won't occur on the open sea. True, someone may get their foot sliced off when the Traveller unexpectedly slams across the mainsheet track. You may occasionally limp into port with a broken boom, torn sails and a gash in her side. ('But what do you expect in a Force 9 with an untrained crew – lucky to get back at all.') You might even lose a child or two en route ('And after I'd kept on telling them to clip themselves on'.) And there's almost bound to be the odd finger that gets crushed in a winch. ('Just one of those 'fings'.') After all, as you'll tell them in the yacht club bar: 'When you sail, you must expect things to happen.' Why do they think there are all those peg-leg sailors around the coast?

The fact is, though, as we pointed out earlier, that cruising keelboats are usually pretty stable, and a real 'deathroll' shouldn't happen. (If it does, and you survive, say it was a 'freak wave'.) The *real* danger faced by the Survival Skipper, however, is to his reputation on casting-off and mooring.

No matter how little sign of life there may be as you sail through that flotilla of gently rocking boats towards your berth, you can be sure there are a hundred pairs of ears and eyes waiting for just one thing – *for you to goof.* The real disasters happen when you're close to home, in the presence of all those 'sailors' who never move their boats off their pontoon.

You can, of course, simply try to avoid these situations. You can limit yourself to night sailing, or you can go out very early in the morning, and come back in after dark. That way, at least, you will spare yourself the comments of that character who is always standing on the end of the jetty during the day and calls out: 'I say, your jib sheet's in the water, you know.'

But, what with the tides (which invariably mean departure at 3.30 – not midnight or 6.30), and the disinclination of many crews to go out at night, the fact is that those daytime incidents, usually bringing you into conflict with other boats, will be almost inevitable.

When this happens, the key rule to observe is: Whatever you do, it was what you *intended* to do. This should get you through a lot of those potentially embarrassing everyday situations that happen to us all. Who has not pulled in to get diesel and been blown stern-on to the dock?

When a third party is involved, Rule number one holds good: *always blame it on them.* And be quite ruthless about it. The Survival Skipper can be hard on his crew; but that's nothing to how hard he can be on people he *doesn't* know. If, for instance, you find a boat on your mooring, you need feel no qualms about casting her adrift. (Anyway they're probably the ones who have skipped off with the dinghy you left on it.)

When entering an unfamiliar port, however, more often than not you will just have to take what you can get. This invariably means closing in, with your fenders down, on a group of boats that are already clustered somewhere. Even in swinging moorings there's going to be a lot of bumping and boring on today's overcrowded waterways. On pier, pontoon or harbour wall, you are likely to find half a dozen or more boats rafted together at the most popular spots – nearest the pub or by the loos. *But don't let this prevent you from going in.*

In any of these multiple mooring situations, there's bound to be some wowser who tries to shoo you off. And even when you've got your boathook well and truly buried in someone else's deck, he's unlikely to leave off. He'll claim that you've got your springs and your breast ropes the wrong way round; or that you are getting everyone else's lines tangled onshore and off; and that one of your lines will pull his pulpit off when the tide goes down. You can safely ignore him, though; or just ask him what he expects if he chooses to buy a Moody with one of those high freeboards.

If he still doesn't give up and goes around untying and retying all your knots, don't let him get away with it. Do them all up again yourself – using, in each case, one of your 'spaghetti specials' (that completely bury the cleat).

Then put him firmly in his place: 'Never seen one of those before – the old Bremerhaven Bight? Looks complicated – but it'll ease with the tide and still stay taut. The bargees in North Germany still use it a lot – you can't hold one of those coal-carriers with just a couple of half hitches.' That should sort him out – no seaman likes to see his knotmanship shown up.

There will be occasions when you may feel it would be easier to simply head up to the 'visitors moorings'. But you'll invariably find that they are situated in the worst possible place. Be wary, too, of what appears to be a genuinely vacant berth – there's bound to be something wrong with it. It'll be where the trawlermen land their catch or by the sewage outfall. No, frequently your only sensible course will be to head straight for one of the good spots, where everyone else is gathered, and not bother with any of that 'permission to come alongside?' nonsense.

But there are more subtle approaches. And it's as well to have a few little tricks up your sleeve – so as not to always have to rely on pure brute force.

For instance, you could try slipping into a handy berth bearing one of those 'reserved' or 'no mooring' signs. Once you've made sure the coast is clear, you simply remove the sign and add it to the collection you keep on board. Then, on the outside of *your* boat, you hang one of your own signs saying 'Ambulance yacht – no mooring alongside' or 'Reserved for Members of the Royal Lebanese Phalangists Yacht Club'. Keeping on board a selection of hand-painted burgees (with a number of them displaying crossed swords or guns) can also come in useful.

Your main object, at this stage, is to deter any other would-be neighbours, who, despite your notices, seem determined to come alongside. For this purpose, it can be worthwhile to train up the kids to start making a racket if another boat approaches – getting one of them perhaps to keep blowing neurotically on the whistle in his life-jacket. Sometimes it's enough just to turn up the radio; or to keep a fierce animal on board; or to say you'll be casting off very early in the morning; or that you are going for a night sail. A small printed sign on the coaming by the hatch, bearing the message 'Victims of Herpes Sailing Party', can also work wonders. Or you could try calling out: 'You wouldn't mind terribly holding off for five minutes would you. You see we're just waiting for our twin rugby club boat, and we're planning a joint deck party. If you'd like to join us, of course, we'd be delighted.'

On some occasions, you'll find yourself having to deal with a club boatman or harbour master trying to move you on and telling you you can't park where you want to. But try not to take too much notice. Just turn up the engine and pretend you can't hear, or hoist your Red Ensign and yellow duster to the crosstrees and pretend to be foreigners who can't understand a word the man says. Once you're securely tied up, you'll be a lot harder to shift.

Sometimes you can even win these officials over with a touch of the amateur dramatics: you get the crew to put on their tattered set of oilies, and appear on deck looking distraught and wailing uncontrollably. You then say: 'Bit of a rough passage I'm afraid, harbour master – hand lost at sea.' Or: 'Would you mind if we just hung on here for a few minutes – sick child on board you know.'

You stand a good chance of avoiding these people altogether, though, if you delay your arrival till after dark (when the marina master will have been replaced by a rather somnolent nightwatchman), and then breeze in, looking as if you belong, pushing off early the next morning before the marina master comes on duty again.

Incidentally, always check back in your log to see what name your boat was sailing under on the last occasion when you berthed in these particular waters. It may be as well to carry a new name this time since harbour masters often have quite a good memory. It helps, therefore, to have a child on board who is handy with the decals or has been trained as a signwriter.

These skills will be indispensable if you're going in for the What-a-Coincidence ploy. This essentially means finding a convenient vacant mooring or pontoon which, let's say, is marked 'Many Splendoured Thing' or 'Reserved for Many Splendoured Thing'. You then put your young sign-writer to work, transforming your own boat into another 'Many Splendoured Thing', thus permitting you to berth with apparent legitimacy.

You have a problem, of course, if the original 'Many Splendoured Thing' now puts in an appearance. You'll just have to say to them words to the effect of: How embarrassing – you wrote to the club secretary giving the itinerary of your cruise, and were simply delighted to find when you arrived that apparently a mooring had been made ready for you. Silly mistake, really – on your part. Still, how charming to find another 'Many Splendoured Thing' on the water. There aren't many of them about. And would they mind terribly if you moored alongside . . .

Often, though, it doesn't pay to be too subtle. Just get in there and make fast. Speed is always of the essence. As we've said, you're a lot harder to shift once you're tied up and your raiding party is ashore, than when you're approaching. Also, of course, the longer you take on a manoeuvre and the more instructions shouted, the more likely it is to go wrong, and the more attention you will draw to yourself. So get your fenders down, position your best long-jumper on the foredeck and just hope you can cut the engine at the right moment. If your timing is a bit off, just mutter something about 'damned seaweed round the shaft – there's no telling which way she'll lurch'.

Don't worry too much about *where* you come alongside. The important thing is to *just make contact.*

For this reason it's advisable to have fenders along the whole length of your boat, as well as on bow and stern. (If queried about this, you can always say it's to protect *your* boat from bad handling by others.) A maxi-sized boathook is also useful for hauling yourself in once you get it hooked round one of the next boat's stanchions. If, by mischance, the stanchion should give way, don't worry too much. Just say to the owner breezily: 'They don't make Nicholsons the way they used to. Lucky that came off now, though. Could have been very dangerous if it went when you were out at sea.'

However much havoc you are wreaking, the important thing is always to look thoroughly pleased with yourselves, confidently calling out instructions to one another ('bearing away', 'full astern', 'hold her steady'), for all the world like one of those composed crews who make a perfect landing every time. If your approach should seem a bit unorthodox, however, just call out 'Well done, crew – now that's what I call a *real* Reverse Admiralty Sweep'.

If you really want to impress, of course, there's always the approach under sail. The drill here is the same: keep your cool – even on a downwind landing with the sails up. And after the crunching has died down, pronounce gamely: 'That's always a risky one, admittedly – but a marvellous feeling when you pull it off.'

Try, incidentally, whenever possible, to come alongside a harbour wall or pontoon, rather than onto a conventional mooring. It does give you the chance to show off your seamanship. And it is such a bore getting out the dinghy, which is sure to be wet. It's also a racing certainty that someone will run off with one of your oars while you're in the pub (so that you'll have to either spend half the night trying to steal someone else's oar, or paddling out with your hands). Besides, anchoring is such a messy business. You never quite know what's going on down there. That phrase '*weigh* anchor' clearly was coined for a very good reason – they can be very heavy things to pull up, even when they're not stuck.

One last point to remember; when you are visiting an unfamiliar port,

always make sure that your own conduct is irreproachable. They may behave unpleasantly towards you, but don't let that prevent you from doing the right thing — always saluting the officers of the club, only flying the ensign when the owner is aboard from sunrise to sunset, and so on.

○ MOORING

The harbour master always says 'No'

The place where you put the fenders will *not* be the place where the hull rubs against the pontoon

If you moor stern-on, you will have forgotten to bring the gangplank

You are more likely to moor on a falling tide

There are never enough mooring warps

Your mooring efforts will be secure only until you leave the boat

The boat moored inside you always will want to put to sea the next morning before you do

6 Navigation

'Where am I now – when I need me?'

Title of George Axelrod novel

As we have seen, much of the fun of cruising comes from getting about, getting to know new people and new places, never quite knowing what may lie ahead of you. But despite the attractions of 'mystery' cruises, it's sometimes nice – and comforting – to know *where* you will be getting about to, *which* new places you will be seeing, and more particularly, what shoals, rocks or sandbanks you may encounter en route. And that's where navigation comes in. Or rather, that's where navigation is *supposed* to come in (since for most Survival Sailors this is a somewhat less than exact science).

As anyone who has ever had a go will know, it's one thing to get it right in navigation class, with the teacher nodding and frowning helpfully to keep your calculations on course. And it's quite another to do it on the open sea, in a horizontally heeling boat, with a helmsman who can't steer a straight course, panic numbing your brain, and waves crashing over the bows, soaking you, your chart and your pencil.

This is why many Survival Skippers prefer to treat navigation as something to keep the intellectual on board amused, while they get on with the serious business of running the ship (pausing only to complain about the intellectual's incompetence when the ship runs aground).

However, it is not always possible to find a member of the crew who is hooked on 'taking a fix' and on taking the blame when things go wrong. And if there is no volunteer, the Survival Skipper will have to make his own calculations – or rather to do his own guesswork. In fact, there are some who would argue that, even with a navigator aboard, getting the boat to where it's supposed to go *is* the skipper's responsibility.

Certainly it can come in very useful to know how to give your exact position on the old ship-to-shore when you 'Mayday' in to the coastguard – thus providing some light relief (that it isn't them) to all the other sailors who are tuned in to Channel 16. (This is, in fact, about the only time you'll be able to get on to the radio-telephone, which at all other times will be hogged by characters making long calls to their wives explaining how they are stuck in a gale off the Scillies and won't be able to get home that night, and then ringing their girlfriends to say they'll be alongside within the hour.)

The Survival Skipper will also feel a lot more confident if he knows where he is – particularly when out of sight of land or in the dark; or rather, if he *thinks* he knows where he is – at night it's all too easy, to confuse the moon (or car headlights and traffic lights on shore) with navigation lights.

Thus, the ambitious Survival Skipper may well find himself having a stab of his dividers at navigation. It should pay off. Even a fairly superficial knowledge can add considerably to his reputation; and, as we've said, he may have little choice but to do his own chartwork, if there's no one else on board who has been to 'nav class'.

The Survival Navigator will be much helped by the mystique which surrounds navigation. It is, as they say, both an art and a science – the art consisting largely of developing 'navigator's hunch', and the science being invaluable for blinding the crew with. There you sit, armed with your dividers and your parallel rulers, 'walking' lines across your chart, totally absorbed in your rhumb lines, ratios and reciprocals, surrounded by Reed's, the pilot, assorted nautical almanacs and numerous sets of tide tables.

The Survival Navigator should always make a point of scrawling down a lot of complicated squiggles and obscure calculations and formulas, as he consults his GHA and Traverse tables, ponders his azimuths and his intercepts, and juggles his cosines and his haversines. This sort of thing can be very impressive to the uninitiated; and, more important, *it can deter the rest of the crew from becoming too curious about what you are actually doing.*

They do say you shouldn't mark your charts, and charts certainly don't come cheap. But this advice is better ignored by the Survival Sailor. It can also pay dividends to strew around the cabin a few well-marked charts of difficult, dangerous and distant voyages which you evidently have negotiated in the past.

However, despite your experience with these earlier passages, you won't always manage to fathom things out on a daysail much closer to home. Fortunately, there are a number of handy terms, presumably invented by other Survival Navigators, which you can blame for any confusion – like compass error or index error (not, you will note, *human* error). Then there are the 'variation' and 'deviation' factors, not to mention the chart itself. ('Damned Admiralty charts – always out of date before they're printed.')

Making excuses is all part of the art of navigation, as is taking it out on your helmsman. The Survival Navigator can always safely take him or her to task, since it is about as impossible to steer a straight course as it is to plot one. So when you're really stumped, you can always storm up on deck shouting: 'Just how much leeway have you been allowing? It's no good simply looking at the sails, you know. You've got to watch the card.'

There will also be occasions – rare, but they do happen – when you do manage to make out the lighthouse or buoy in front of you. (It won't be the one you wanted to see – but never mind.) Thus you may be in the happy position of being able to tell your crew exactly where you are going – or, at least, to draw a tentative conclusion as to your whereabouts. If it takes you a while to identify the buoy by the colour and its markings, and you have to dilly-dally, simply put on your 'do not disturb me now' look and say: 'Just looking for a safety bearing to come in on.'

Until you get to this point, though, it's as well to maintain a studied vagueness about the whole proceedings, and not to make any rash predictions. To any questions about the finer points (like 'Where are we?', 'Where are we heading?', 'Should we be bumping into those lobster pots?'), simply fog the issue with a few of the more abstruse navigational terms, look superior, and say condescendingly: 'Now who's doing the navigating – you or me?'

It's even best not to let on even if, perchance, you *do* know where you are. (The Newhaven–Dieppe ferries may have just crossed, and among your tables – concealed from view – is one showing the departure time of both vessels, enabling you to work out exactly where they (and you) are – assuming that both boats left on time.) Far better, though, to let your crew sweat it out.

It's on these occasions that you can confidently make your course sound a lot more adventurous than it really is. You can point out the sandbank about 100 yards to port, or draw their attention to some nasty little submerged rocks or wrecks. See a couple of birds perched on the water not far off, and you say, with a wink: 'They're not walking on water those gulls you know.' Or: 'Didn't you see that cardinal marker on the reef – you've got to keep your eyes peeled, you know, old son.'

You can, of course, generally do this with more aplomb if you've carefully chosen a course with a minimum of hazards, which permits the maximum possible deviation from the route without running into trouble. For, as any navigator knows, 'variation' and 'deviation' is what it's all about. Even when you're not all that sure of yourself, try not to let it show. Don't let the others see that you're rattled even though, according to your 'calculations', you should have got there by now.

One way of maximising your chances is to pick a big enough target area – France, for instance, which has a long enough coastline and is not too far away. Try, nevertheless, to aim for the *middle* of it; otherwise you may miss it altogether and find yourself in the Azores. You can't be too careful. And do make sure that it *is* France before putting up your courtesy flag. French seagulls do look pretty much like Belgian seagulls – or English ones, for that matter. It is just possible that you confused the Newhaven–Dieppe ferry with the Dover–Ostend – or perhaps even the Ostend–Dover. (It can be a bit embarrassing calling out in broken French to a gang of English fishermen.)

So keep your cool, even when you suspect that ferry should have been sailing in the other direction; or that you may have just missed the headland; or that those swimmers were speaking in *German* (and might be in home waters, rather than on holiday in France or in the UK). Incidentally, never stoop to asking such people where you are – nor for that matter, divers, fishermen or other vessels. Do, however, keep your ears open: a shout of 'Merde alors, capitaine!' from a fishing boat you have just bumped into is a fair indication that you are nearing French waters.

It's also worthwhile, on occasion, 'adjusting' your course to follow another boat that looks as if she knows where she's going – provided she's not going too fast. There's usually something purposeful about a boat that's on course and heading for home (another example of where 'navigator's hunch' comes in). If this boat looks like slipping away from you, you can, of course, always start to motor, on the pretext that if you don't 'we'll miss the tidal gate' and 'God knows how long it'll all take if that happens'.

Switching to motor probably won't meet with too many objections from the crew. The prospect of spending any longer than necessary on the water (with you) won't be too appealing, and they will probably want to keep it to a minimum. In fact, the most frequent question which the crew will put to the navigator is, 'how much longer?', followed by, once you have arrived, 'why did it take so long?'

The fact is, it always takes longer than you think – even when you have an objective in view. So avoid giving ETAs. Far better to reply: 'You see, it depends so much. Here, take a look at this.' You then point to a page in one of your tables, ramble on a bit about isogonals and the vector scale and Mercator's projection, and remind them that you can never eliminate 'deviation' altogether, even without the effect of tides, winds and currents, not to mention the fact that the 'variation' *differs* just at the point where you are sailing.

Of course, you may have to polish up your story a bit at the yacht club bar later if it's a case of explaining why you were more than ten hours late getting from Shoreham to Chichester: 'Ran into an amazing contraflow slippery surface sea area – must have had six knots against under the hull.' One more tip: always turn back the log quickly at the end of the voyage so the others won't know how far you *actually sailed* in order to get from A to B or, more likely, from A to Z.

The important thing is to get there in the end; or, at least, to get *somewhere* in the end. So keep going. With any luck, sooner or later, something recognisable will heave into sight. It may not be what you expected, or what you rashly predicted, in which case, if anyone expresses surprise, you say: 'Didn't I tell you – we changed course three hours out. Otherwise we'd have been caught scraping the bar or been taken by the current, and what with the tide about to turn . . . surely you felt the wind shift?' There are even occasions – admittedly rare – when a landmark turns up exactly as anticipated; and you now have the problems of avoiding the buoy rather than finding it.

The less ambitious Survival Navigator, however, may prefer to stay within sight of the coast. It does make you feel more secure – even in those bad weather conditions when you are supposed to head out to sea, away from the rocks and eddies. There is something comforting about keeping some tall cliffs in view.

The coastline can be deceptive at times, though – one piece of cliff does tend to look much like another piece of cliff. It does help, therefore, to do your homework beforehand – ideally hiring a helicopter so that you can familiarise yourself with piers and promontories, and other significant features along the coast. Alternatively, you can stick to the same stretch of coast that you always sail. That way you will *know* that when the lighthouse is in transit with the gasworks, by steering 200° you should clear the mudbanks. If this doesn't seem very adventurous, one possibility is to sail just out of sight of land – *to the naked eye*. Then, from time to time, when no one is looking, you sneak a quick look at the shore with a well-hidden pair of binoculars or telescope.

There is a good deal to be said for using these traditional methods – not least to enhance the Survival Sailor's reputation ashore as a bit of an old seadog. It's worth making a point, therefore, of always wandering around at the club with a pair of dividers sticking out of your breast pocket. At the office, keep a pair of parallel rulers lying on your desk, along with a brass ship's barometer: 'Just like to keep an eye on that low coming in over Cornwall, old boy. Taking the wife and kids out this weekend.' (It's also worth, on the quiet, listening to the weather forecasts of professional meteorologists – a foggy day at sea feels a lot less romantic than a foggy day in London town.)

Old seadog that you are, however, you won't have much time for some of the new electronic devices. 'Don't know what sailing's coming to with all these new-fangled gadgets. The sport will be full of computer-programmers next.' (It already is.)

In reality, however, the Survival Sailor would be unwise to neglect the benefits of Decca/AP, Loran-C or whatever. He may hold forth at the bar: 'Decca – wouldn't touch it with a bargepole. Give me a parallel rule and a pair of dividers any day, and I'll get you there by the seat of me pants'. But in practice he will have one of these machines surreptitiously installed – carefully concealing the aerial.

He can pretend to his crew that it's some sort of back-up radio, and switch on only when no one is watching to trap those coastal radio signals that by some electronic wizardry show up your position in longitude and latitude on that little screen. This, of course, can be of great help to the Survival Navigator's efforts to locate himself on the blue part of the chart. (With any luck the Japanese should soon be miniaturising them, so that you will even be able to wear one as a watch.)

Thus, the Survival Sailor, on occasion, can just lower his sails when he's out of sight and motor in by Decca, leaving himself ample time at the club bar to tell it like it wasn't: 'Tricky bit of navigation, I'll admit. Still, keeps you up to scratch. Must have been some sort of interference. Compass all over the place and RDF on the blink. But good old dead reckoning got us home as usual. Reminds me of that time when the log went and I came in just using a sextant, rigging up my watch as a sort of compass.'

That's another thing that navigation is all about – nostalgia. And it won't be long before you and your chums are reminiscing once again about the 'old days', before Decca and 'separation zones', when British boats would go round the coast watching British lights, taking 'hand-bearing fixes' off lighthouses, and chatting to the coastguard.

○ NAVIGATION

Navigation doesn't mean you know where you are

If you think you can see Littlehampton, but your calculations say it's Chichester, it's Littlehampton

A nautical mile varies in length according to the speed at which you are travelling

The wrong buoy is better than no buoy

It always looks nearer on the chart

The place you are heading for will always be on *another* chart

The chart is never up to date

When a cup of coffee spills on the chart table, it will invariably blot out precisely that section you will need when you hit fog

---

7 Survival Crewing

**'So we drawed a lot, and accordin' shot
The captain for our meal'**

The Yarn of the *Nancy Bell*, W. S. Gilbert

Of course, the Survival Sailor won't always be able to take charge of the boat. There may be someone aboard who can sail a bit. Or the owner may absolutely *insist* on playing skipper himself.

At times a Survival Sailor may even *choose* not to captain the craft – it is, after all, the skipper who is normally held responsible for all damage and destruction caused, whatever the failings of his crew. In fact, there are a few advantages to being crew rather than captain. And the Survival Sailor should make the most of them. Leading the mutiny, for instance, can be quite fun.

There may also be occasions when you will decide to hire a professional skipper, in which case, you will certainly want to ensure that he earns his money. But even though *he* is the captain, and *you* are the crew, he should, of course, be duly humble about it. You're not paying the piper for nothing.

Be careful, however, about hiring a skipper if you've just bought a new boat. You can be sure that he will start off by telling you about all the additional things you need to buy (navigation equipment and so forth) in order to make the vessel seaworthy. He's also likely to point out a lot of the boat's other shortcomings that you would rather not have known about.

In fact, as crew, your priorities with regard to equipping a boat are invariably different from those of the skipper, who is almost bound to be far too ambitious – in all respects. Skippers, for instance, like Nelson, don't like to neglect a fair wind. So he'll always be wanting to push on all the time. And this means keeping you and your shipmates constantly busy on deck – with mooring practice, or stripping the engine, as your only light relief. He simply won't appreciate that you and your comrades have too many *other* things to worry about without constantly hauling the sails up and down.

The first concern of a good Survival Crewman or Crewwoman should always be the comfort and well-being of themselves and of their fellow 'rovers'. Be wary, therefore, of the sort of boat which has charts under every berth. It's true that most chart-tables hold only twenty-five charts – but that should be more than sufficient for the amount of sailing you'll be doing, (if *you* have anything to do with it).

So see to it that the storage space under the bunks is used for bottles of booze. Don't let the skipper give you any of that nonsense about 'keeping a dry ship'. How else are you going to be able to drink the loyal toast (which, fortunately, on boats, you are allowed to drink sitting down)? How else are you and your shipmates going to be able to keep up their morale – even if this might result in giving your ship a reputation which would earn it a mention in 'Jane's Fighting Drunks'.

Booze is also about the only way of disguising the taste (if that's the word) of what you'll be eating; and it will often provide a very welcome alternative. The word 'mess' to describe where meals are taken in the navy is not at all inapt. For whatever else boats may be about, it is not *haute cuisine*. Don't be surprised if instant mashed potato and strawberry jam eaten with a teaspoon turn out to be the gastronomic high point of your voyage. And your basic diet will consist of the contents of anonymous tins (the labels wash off in the bilges) which will be fished out periodically. (You eat at very odd times on boats.)

This will, however, be preferable to having someone aboard who pretends to be a bit of a cook. That will inevitably mean that this person – undeterred by the capacity of your gimballing cooker to 'loop the loop' – will insist on 'having a go'. And even if she (it's usually a she) does manage to concoct something halfway edible, you can be very sure that it will be precisely as she's on the point of ladling it out that the skipper – suddenly discovering that he's on a collision course – will violently tack the boat.

Even under less extreme circumstances, cooking on board requires very considerable gymnastic ability and lightning reactions – to lie on your back peering into what is laughably called an oven, but which would fit five times inside a microwave; and to catch in mid-air the pots that come flying off that rocking flame-thrower that passes for a hot stove, and is liable to explode at any minute. 'Proper' cooking, of course, also means more washing up. And that tiny bowl of greasy water (salt water at that) can only handle so many stained plastic plates and burned pots and pans.

So spare your volunteer cook the trouble. The stench in the cabin will be bad enough anyway without overloading the gash bag. There'll be the smell of seaweed and sewage at low tide, not to mention the whiff of those of your shipmates who always change into their pyjamas but never change their socks. And the smell of food (and bottled gas) does tend to *mingle* with clothes.

You may not think too much about this when you set out. After all, you tell yourself, you'll be spending most of your time on deck enjoying the sea, the sun and the fresh air. That's certainly the way they make it look in the ads — beautiful people lounging on the sundeck, looking tanned and fit. That's cruising for you — good food, invigorating air, convivial company. *You* won't be spending much time in the cabin. The fact is though that, as it turns out, the cabin may well be preferable to a wet deck on a cold night with a forty-knot draught blowing across it.

In general, life on a cruising yacht is much less healthy than is often imagined. You'll get 'yachtsman's stoop' from spending all that time hunched up in the well. And your eating and sleeping routines will be completely disrupted. It's not for nothing that yachtsmen tend to suffer from piles and constipation.

What with this, and all the other little things that are sent to try us on a boat, it does pay, therefore, for the Survival Sailor to pick his fellow crew members very carefully. You need people with a range of separate skills, who will fall into clearly defined roles: someone with A-level maths to navigate; someone who can read and write to keep the log; a short-order cook to make the beer and sandwiches; keen youngsters for the foredeck; and for the motor and the loo, a marine engineer who is prepared to spend hours buried in the bilges unblocking the circulating pump. (Always praise this man's ingenuity by the way — 'you'll have to show me how you do it one of these days'.)

By handpicking this sort of équipe (though it's not *always* possible) the Survival Sailor should thus have a crew where mutual dependence is the order of the day, thereby forging those 'tight bonds' of a group of people who sail together — *and whose collective skills should exempt the Survival Sailor from any of the more taxing tasks.*

Not that there won't be disputes — even among a very close-knit team. After all, it's only natural that tempers should fray and small niggles become amplified in tiring cramped conditions. And this is where the Survival Crewman can come into his own. If, for instance, there's any aggro between skipper and crew, the Survival Crewman can step in as a sort of unofficial shop steward, calming things down, and insisting that the skipper now heaves-to so that you can all break open another bottle — or three.

The Survival Crewman should not underestimate the importance of this role of keeping the team together. It can be vital — particularly if you are going to corroborate one another's stories when you fetch up back at the club.

The Survival Sailor can also do his bit to keep up morale on board. Make a point, for example, of taking each of your comrades aside, in turn and individually, to compliment them on how well they are doing: 'You know, you're really the one who keeps this thing going. I can't see why *you* aren't the skipper – at least you know something about it.'

This will give them all a bit of a lift, making them think all the more highly of you, and making them that much less likely to suggest that you might just not be pulling your weight.

○ NIGHT WATCHING

Your relief watch never arrives on time

You will be asked to take over on time

The snacks for the watch will have been finished by the watch immediately preceding yours

You'll feel more like sleeping when you're on watch than when you're down below

If you do nod off, the worst will happen

The only time anything ever happens is when *you're* on watch

It will be impossible to return to your bunk after your watch without waking at least one other person

---

8 Relief at Sea

'We have all passed a lot of water since then'

Sam Goldwyn

One thing that is almost certainly going to cause friction between skipper/ owner and crew is use of 'the heads'. Or, rather, if the skipper has his way – *non-use* of the heads. Most owners make no secret of the fact that they'd rather you 'didn't go'; and many will go to great lengths to prevent the Survival Crewman from performing that most basic of bodily functions in the manner to which he or she is accustomed.

Curiously enough, this is one of the aspects of life afloat that is rarely discussed in any detail in the standard textbooks. And yet, there can be little doubt that on most yachts the use of the loo is about the most complex operation a sailor has to perform. It is certainly the one most likely to go wrong.

Much of the aggravation between captain and crew stems from the fact that this is one of the few tasks on board that boat-owners are not able to supervise personally. Not that they won't try. If they could, they'd probably get in there with you. And you'll almost certainly be subjected to a discreet toilet-training lecture. Some skippers even post a large notice just inside or outside that fetid little cabinet giving detailed instructions about how to use the thing.

These notices, however, can be safely ignored by the Survival Crewman. Even if you follow the instructions to the letter, the plumbing will never perform as it should. The reality is that all nautical loos get blocked, and leak, and will accept a minimum of organic waste. Whatever the manufacturers may claim, boat loos simply don't work – never mind the 'extras', like 'battery-operated pressure-sensitive seats which eliminate odour'.

Despite all the advances in marine technology, most yacht loos won't even accept toilet paper, what with the small bore of the tubes and all the other obstacles which waste has to negotiate – swan necks, pistons, sea-cocks, valves, flaps and so on.

One problem is that no two boat loos, like marine engines, are alike – hence the owner's conviction that *he* is the only one who understands its little idiosyncrasies. Some things, though, they do all have in common: the levers always come off in your hands; the plastic parts simply get eaten away by any normal chemical toilet; the seat will never stay up without being held - and you need your hands, of course, for other things. Many of them are not even very securely attached to the cabin sole – with the result that you can find yourself being hurled into the corner cradling the pan in your arms.

Nonetheless, there will be times when the Survival Crewman will feel it's time to go. And if that's the case, don't let the owner put you off. You can be pretty certain he'll try. If he sees you seeking out the convenience (they're often well hidden), there'll be the shout of 'You have read the instructions, haven't you?' Best just to say you have, or he'll try to blind you with science, and perhaps offer a veiled threat that if you block it he'll make you repair it. (The skipper may forgive you for not knowing how to reef, but he'll never forgive you for blocking his loo.)

Some skippers will even try to plead with you: 'Couldn't you perhaps try to hold on till the marina? Only another couple of hours.' ('Holding on', incidentally, is the main cause of that particular style of sailor's walk often seen around the marina known as 'the knock-kneed mince' as yachtsmen make a beeline from their boats towards the portacabins.)

The Survival Crewman, however, should not allow himself to be reduced to this state. Don't let the skipper put you off with remarks like 'I'm afraid the head may be locked – not sure where I put the key'. And if he's tried to be clever by jamming the door, the Survival Crewman will just have to take a screwdriver to it.

So make sure you stand your ground. When a Survival Sailor's gotta go, he's gotta go. So any remarks about penalties that may be incurred for 'blocking the head' should be simply answered by telling the skipper that at least unblocking it will provide him with something to occupy his time when he gets ashore.

Having asserted your basic human rights, however, you can be sure that won't be the end of the story. The skipper is unlikely to simply resign himself to the worst (which is almost bound to happen). He'll probably try one or two other ploys: 'Better hurry up Richard. I'll be tacking in two minutes'; or, 'Stand by below, looks like a strong squall up ahead'.

He may even enlist the aid of the rest of the crew, and, just as you've installed yourself, get them all scrambling noisily around on deck preparing for some complicated manoeuvre, and bellowing out: 'Where on earth has he got to? Doesn't he realise we're trying to sail a boat up here? We can't do it all on our own.'

The Survival Crewman, needless to say, should simply ignore all this and concentrate on the job in hand. If you do succumb to his blandishments, it will just make your own problems worse. And they'll probably be bad enough already – since in all likelihood the attitude of the skipper, combined with your own attempts to 'hold on' will have resulted in a severe case of 'nervous retention'.

You'll find it hard enough to concentrate on what you're doing anyway. Your mind will almost certainly be elsewhere – probably trying to work out where they've hidden the toilet paper (usually in the stern locker). Chances are you'll also be in a state of mild concussion as a result of banging your nut on the deckhead, which won't make it any easier to remember the instructions.

Five minutes earlier the theory of it all may have seemed delightfully simple. Just a question of opening the seacock and pumping the water in; then pumping the water out and closing the seacock. The fact is, though, that in no other nautical operation is theory so much at variance with practice. The likelihood is that either you'll close everything and pump and the water will just continue to rise; or your pumping will succeed in draining, but you'll fail utterly to get any water back in.

Going through all this rigmarole won't be made any easier by your skipper, who, having failed at verbal intimidation, will now in all probability be working on other methods to dislodge you. Thus, just when you think the boat is heeling the right way so you can pump correctly, the skipper will perform some dramatic change of course so thwarting your best efforts. As if it wasn't hard enough to pump the bowl full of water without breaking the handle. You also can be sure that whatever safety device may be fitted to control the flush, there's bound to be that rush of water into the pan at the most inconvenient moment.

The skipper's attitude is in some ways understandable, stemming — as we've said — from sheer frustration at not being able to control this operation. It wasn't always so, of course. In the old days when 'bucket and chuck it' was the only system available, the owner could keep an eye on things, or give the order *not* to keep an eye on things — telling the crew to 'all face aft', particularly when the ladies went about their business.

Happily, however, these days the Survival Crewman who keeps his cool can do his own thing, *without* any help from his friends. Another point well worth bearing in mind is that it pays *to do your own thing first*. The fact is that it's advisable to make use of the facilities while they are still in working order. So don't let yourself succumb to any of that machismo nonsense about not wanting to be the first one to crack. If needs must, get in there first — *it may be your last chance.*

Whatever disaster may strike you in the head though, the important thing is to keep your own head about you when you reemerge. On no account should the Survival Crewman accept any blame for those inevitable cock-ups which occurred inside.

Your best plan is probably to insinuate that someone surreptitiously got in there before you and didn't own up to the havoc caused — 'the blackguard'. Or, perhaps, that the owner hadn't made sure the briny-closet was working properly before you set out. So tell him straight: 'When I leave port, I like to think I'm on a vessel that's shipshape.'

That, of course, may not be the end of the story. If you're making a longish passage, you may well find that you'll have to pay a return visit down there at some stage. Hence the importance — as we stressed in the previous chapter — of picking your fellow crewmen carefully. Do try to make sure that the marine engineer on board knows how to fix the damn thing. And equally important, that he *is willing to do so* — some mechanics do show a certain reluctance to get involved in that department.

If the worst does come to the worst, though, there is at least one small consolation: the characters who race in those ultimate sailing machines, won't be any better off than you are. In fact, the nautical loo in its purest form is to be found in the super light hulls of the IOR fleet where it will be installed in isolated splendour in its plastic covering in the most inaccessible part of the boat.

Incidentally, should the Survival Sailor, by recklessness or mischance, find himself aboard one of these vessels he should avoid displaying his ignorance by remarks like: 'Bit difficult to get at, isn't it?' For whilst IOR rules require the loo, they do *not* require the hole through the hull – which will rarely be provided. ('Think of the drag, old boy.')

The owners of those Whitbread round-the-world boats have gone even further. Only too aware of the dangers of seacocks bursting and letting in vast quantities of water miles from land, they've set up their lavatory seats on deck, bolted to the pushpit (not the pulpit!), complete with toilet rolls and vanity curtains – the quintessential 'loo with a view'. How better to contemplate the mysteries of the deep than with the house-high rollers of the South Atlantic all around you, a healthy fifty-knot wind across the deck to provide a little ventilation, and 2,500 fathoms of the Tasman basin beneath your posterior?

○ THE HEADS

At the heads, you lose

The head works fine till someone uses it

No one ever admits to blocking the heads

There will be more people on board capable of blocking the heads than there are capable of fixing them

The toilet paper will never be kept in the head

If the pump fills the bowl, it won't empty it

If the pump empties the bowl, it won't fill it

Following the 'instructions for use' to the letter will lead to a complete blockage of the pipework

---

9 Sailsmanship

**'I unrolled the sail. It seemed a complicated job, but I
accomplished it at length, and then came the question,
which was the top end?'**

Jerome K. Jerome, *Three Men in a Boat*

Whilst the heads constitute one of the main causes of aggravation between owner and crew below decks, out on top it's probably going to be the sails that cause the most trouble. They will, after all, have cost him a bit; and much as he'll enjoy barking out instructions to his crew to keep getting them up and down, this is inevitably going to mean that much more wear and tear. Not a factor to be neglected, these days, with a hi-tech, low-stretch main costing about as much as a fleet of Mirror dinghies.

If the Survival Sailor happens to be the owner, and economy is a factor, you'll just have to find other things to keep the crew busy: perhaps a bit of man overboard practice; or getting them all to untie and retie their knots; or using a leadline instead of the echo-sounder. Finding people things to do is never much of a problem on board.

At the same time, however, it's important to make out that *you are desperate to get more canvas up aloft*. That is, after all, what sailing is all about. So you'll need a handy set of excuses for not sailing fully rigged and making good use of the wind. Try: 'I'd like to hoist the kite when we free off after the headland, but I think we should wait for the 6 o'clock forecast' (said at 3.00 pm).

This approach will also suit the Survival Skipper who is less confident than he might be, and is reluctant to get 'em up on a gusty day in case things get out of hand. After all, the sails are the engine of the boat and they do require a degree of knowledge and skill in hoisting and trimming.

When the welly is on the other foot, and you find yourself in the role of Survival Crewman, your approach in fact will be much the same. *You'll be trying to have as little to do with those sails as possible.* But this won't always work out and there is a danger that you too will get roped in to help.

If this looks like being the case, you can always try to dissuade the Skipper from getting too carried away. You may even be fortunate enough to be sailing with a bit of a Survival Skipper – in which case, the yacht will probably be seen cruising around in eight knots of wind with one reef in the main and the number three jib. ('Just in case it blows up'.)

It'll be a different story, though, with a macho owner who knows a thing or two. Your efforts to persuade him *not* to hoist that huge number one genoa, even with a strengthening wind and a forecast of Force 8, will probably prove in vain. And it may well be that all you'll earn is contempt with your whines about how it isn't that much fun being hanked on to the pulpit in a howling gale trying to tear down 300 square feet of flogging salt-caked Dacron.

You can, of course, try to enlist the support of your fellow crewmen, but they simply may not be willing to follow your Mr Christian to his Captain Bligh. So you may have no choice but to join the rest of the sail-changing team. If you know what you're about, though, it needn't be all that bad — as we shall see.

First, you can try to limit your involvement with hoisting and lowering *by busying yourself with the sail-locker.* So look sharp and volunteer to fetch the new sail that the skipper is screaming for. This sail will, in fact, invariably be somewhere at the bottom of the locker buried by all the other sail-bags and spare junk that will have been tossed in there.

With any luck, too, the locker will be down in *the stern out of sight, behind the skipper's back* and well away from the rest of the team on the foredeck. This will give the Survival Sailor plenty of scope for noisily shifting a few of the upper bags around and complaining loudly about the disorderly way they've been stowed, and even suggesting that some silly bugger must have stowed some of the sails in the wrong bags. You can then open up one or two of the ones that are easier to get at, and perhaps — when you've got one or two of your shipmates looking in your direction — upend yourself into the locker, with just your legs sticking out, making it look as if you are trying to get at the sail-bag at the bottom that everyone is clamouring for. *On no account, however, should you try to extract this particular bag.* This could result in a bad case of double hernia, or at the very least, severe groin strain.

The secret is to keep up your performance long enough for one or two of your foredeck sail-mates to come to your assistance. You can then allow them to locate and extract the bag they're after (while you are rooting around in the opposite corner of the locker). Do make sure though to offer them your congratulations: 'Well done chaps, I knew it had to be in there somewhere.'

The trick, now, if you want to avoid any involvement with hoisting the damn thing, is to *stick with the locker.* Say out loud, making sure the skipper hears: 'So I suppose I'm the poor sod who is going to have to sort this lot out. I do take it you like to have the *right* sails in the *right* bags, eh, skip?' Thus, you should be able to continue with your 'sorting out' until the rest of the crew have finished jumping to it on the foredeck.

Of course, this won't always work. Someone may beat you to the locker. Or the skipper may decide to deploy you elsewhere. If that's the case, here are a few tips on actual 'sail-handling'.

○ THE MAIN ○

Normally quite a straightforward sail for the Survival Crewman to 'handle' – unless it comes to reefing that is. The golden rule here is to keep well away from the mast. The ideal position is hanging on to the backstay with a stock of tools and winch-handles at the ready. (In the event that the handles, marline spike or screwdriver are actually needed, you can always hand them to someone else who is 'better positioned'.) Do your best, though, to be *involved* with the whole proceedings. So while the others sweat the thing up, keep throwing in the odd useful comment: 'Easy, you chaps. Mind you clear the runners'; or, 'I'll stay here and ease the backstay to power up the main'; or, looking up at the sail and saying knowingly: 'Terrible cut isn't it?'

Once the sail is aloft and the operation is to all intents and purposes completed, the Survival Crewman can leap into action. You can now proceed to the mast, and make a bit of a show at pressing the straining sail with your fingers looking for 'luff tension' and calling for 'more Cunningham'.

We won't tackle the subject of reefing here – simply because this is something the Survival Crewman *should on no account tackle*. Just find some excuse to go below – any excuse; or succumb to a sudden bout of seasickness.

○ THE FORESAILS ○

Jibs, genoas, 'floaters' and the rest may not prove quite so easy for the Survival Sailor to 'handle' as the main. For a start, what with all those corners, you may have difficulty remembering which bit goes where. There also tends to be rather a lot of wet and uncomfortable squatting or kneeling on deck. The Survival Crewman, therefore, may choose to be a bit less involved with foresail work than he is with the main.

The best way to achieve this is to let it be known that you're a bit of a dab-hand as a 'tweaker'. Thus you'll be able to remain in the cockpit with the halyard winch 'ready to go'.

As with 'locker-work', though, *do get in there first.* As soon as the skipper tells the foresail team to get cracking, say to your shipmate: 'I'll tail for you, if you like, Peter – it's easier to see how she's setting from down here.' This should ensure that it's the hapless Peter who gets to work on the winch while you do the watching from the lee rail.

Never let it be thought, however, that you wouldn't be up to the job up front. Make a point, as soon as you see the foredeck crew getting into a tangle attaching the sheets and making the correct bowlines, of calling out crisply: 'Come on now. The rat goes up the hole, round the tree, and back down the hole.' Said with the right air of bored vexation, this should suggest that you could sort it all out with one hand if your sail-trimming skills were not more valuable elsewhere.

Now it is just possible that you won't be able to avoid getting roped in, and that you turn out not to know quite so much about sail-setting as you claimed. However, if you keep your wits about you, all need not be lost. If, for instance, you commit a real bloomer and hoist a jib tack overhead, just call out to the astonished skipper: 'Nice one, eh, skip? Recent studies do show this can often tighten the leech and provide more drive.' In fact you can hoist just about anything 'to provide more drive' – sleeping bags or even an umbrella (like a recent Fastnet winner who used to ask his crew to hoist a black brolly along with the spinnaker when running his GP14 downwind in his dinghy racing days).

○ **THE SPINNAKER** ○

A synonym for trouble – expensive trouble at that. The best way to limit your involvement with this one, is probably simply to remind the skipper/owner of the price tag: 'Beautiful sail, that new 0.5 oz Triradial, Tony. But don't you think there may just be a *tiny* bit too much wind. It'd be a pity to pull her out of shape. What do these things cost now, as a matter of interest?' Chances are, particularly if the crew haven't exactly got their act together with the standard foresails, that 'skip' may well decide to boom out the genoa after all.

That isn't to say that the Survival Crewman – or the Survival Skipper, for that matter – should avoid the spinnaker entirely. The time to display her though, in all her glorious Technicolor is back at the marina 'drying out' (even though she may not have been used). Obviously there's no point in spending all that money if you can't show her off.

On board, too, the Survival Crewman can put spinnakers to some use. If he's succeeded in putting himself in charge of the sail-locker, he can spend a great deal of time folding or unfolding them and checking the gear – particularly at those moments when the rest of the crew are engaged in more onerous duties.

You may even find that by lavishing so much admiration and affection on the pride of the skipper's sail-locker that you find yourself going up in his estimation. He may even give you the benefit of the doubt when it comes to deciding on your competence or incompetence. After all, someone who seems to love his kaleidoscopic kite almost as much as you do can't be *all* bad.

○ SPINNAKERS

The best place to fly the spinnaker is at the marina

In a race, any extra speed gained by using a spinnaker will not make up for the time and hassle of hoisting it

The winches you are using for the spinnaker sheets are always the ones you need for something else

The newer the spinnaker, the more likely it is to rip

It's best to take the spinnaker down before you broach

You never do

The boat in front of you *without* a spinnaker will be going faster

The boat behind you *with* a spinnaker *also* will be going faster

Spinnakers are as good at slowing a boat down when trailing in the water as they are at making the boat go faster

---

10 Points of Sailing

**'There's something wrong with our bloody ships today,
Chatfield. Steer two points nearer the enemy.'**

Vice-Admiral Beatty, at the Battle of Jutland

The Survival Crewman should also go up in his skipper's estimation if he can show that he knows what it's all about when it comes to those classic 'points of sailing'. It's also rather important for the Survival Crewman's own sake that he should know how to handle himself to best advantage when beating, reaching and running. So let's take 'the points' in turn.

○ BEATING TO WINDWARD ○

It's during this phase that the Survival Crewman must really show what he's made of. Offshore, in anything above a Force 4, the boat of course will be heeling markedly in the sort of waves and wind that are definitely not for the faint-hearted. The fact is, though, that — frightening as this situation may seem to a novice — *you are probably better off up top than you would be down below.*

Here then is the chance for the Survival Sailor to indulge in a few heroics: 'Don't worry, George — you stay down in the cockpit' (where it will probably be a damn sight wetter). Meanwhile, before starting the 'work' to windward, the Survival Sailor (well wrapped-up in his triple-lined jacket, woolly hat, scarf and goggles, and equipped with a couple of hip flasks) will have installed himself on the most comfortable spot on the weather-rail (perhaps sitting on a little plastic cushion he's brought along for the purpose).

Once there, though, *on no account should you move from that station —* even during that flurry of activity on board as you approach the weather mark. The Survival Crewman can, however, make a semblance of leaning this way and that, or holding his hands out 'to compensate'. If the skipper calls for a reef or wants to tighten the genoa halyard or the boom outhaul, just tell him: 'Like to help, skip — but don't you think I should keep my weight here or we'll lose vital righting moment.'

○ THE REACH ○

On the reach, the boat should be rather more stable, and more vertical than on the beat (at least without the spinnaker). Here then, after his heroic performance to windward, the Survival Crewman can once again display his spirit of self-sacrifice – offering to go below and make the others some tea. Do make a point, though, of disappearing below fairly promptly – since it's on the reach that the skipper may well make the mistake of raising the kite (which the Survival Sailor may prefer to leave to the others).

Then, having fortified himself with a few drams down in the cabin, the Survival Sailor can reemerge just before the leeward mark with those piping warm mugs of tea to earn the grateful comments of his comrades ('What a fine fellow he is').

○ THE RUN ○

In light airs, when the spinnaker will almost certainly be going up, the drill for the Survival Sailor is to take up his favoured position sitting on the transom, hanging on to the backstay, offering as usual his invaluable advice: 'Is the pole high enough?'; 'Give it a bit more air now'; 'Don't sail too high, skip'; 'Let it breathe'.

In heavy airs, a different approach is called for. Downwind running with the spinnaker is about the most hair-raising experience of all – canvas straining, twelve knots under the boat, half a ton on each line, crew desperate to keep the boat from broaching. In this sort of situation *the Survival Sailor has only one option* – to disappear below into his sleeping bag. As usual, though, he should make it clear that he's only doing this in everyone's best interests: 'I think I'd better get forward, skip. After all, I am about the heaviest on board and we don't want the transom to drag.'

11 Avoidance Crewing

'Some are born lazy, some have idleness thrust upon them'

Beryl Downing, in *The Times*, 1980

Needless to say, not all novice Survival Crewman will manage to pick up the finer 'points of sailing' straightaway. This is certainly nothing to be ashamed of. There's no sense in trying to run before you can walk. If this is the case, therefore, you may need some sort of fallback position – basically enabling you to opt out of crewing entirely when necessary.

The drawback, of course, is that this may not do a great deal for your reputation. But at times 'avoidance crewing' may be the only sensible option. And even experienced Survival Crewmen, in extreme situations, have been known to 'cop out' on board. There's no doubt that this can certainly make your cruise a good deal more agreeable. And you can also derive a good deal of enjoyment from 'rebuilding' your reputation in the bar afterwards – though this can come a bit expensive.

If you do find yourself opting for the cop out approach, you'd do best simply to make it clear right from the start that boats are not something you know a great deal about, and that you are going to be about as much use on board as a chocolate teapot. To make the point, you might turn up, for instance, with your bag of golf clubs. ('Had hoped to get in a little putting practice on the foredeck.')

It may also be as well to appear a little delicate – arriving on board with your hot-water bottle conspicuously displayed. And there's nothing wrong with seeming a little nervous – perhaps bringing along a gigantic distress flag in your holdall, or insisting on lashing yourself down to at least three points if ever you happen to find yourself on deck.

Once under way, try to ensure that the normal pattern of your life will be interrupted as little as possible by shipboard routines. Tell your comrades that you are really looking forward to taking your turn on watch the first night – but you feel, in all fairness, that you should point out that you are slightly colour-blind – 'particularly when it comes to distinguishing red and green'.

However, while you may deselect yourself for most jobs, do see to it that you select for yourself a well-placed berth (as far away as possible from the

heads and galley area). After all, you'll be spending a lot of time on your bunk. Your best bet is probably the largest berth in the saloon, as close as possible to where the booze is stored. No need to join that unseemly scramble when boarding to bag the fo'c's'le – this is actually where the worst shipboard smells linger longest, and it also means you'll probably have to sleep in a sort of banana curve.

It's important, though, not to let these sorts of priorities be misinterpreted by the others. So try to show your goodwill as soon as you step on board, ingratiating yourself by volunteering to do the chores. Make sure, however, that your very first batch of sandwiches ensures your rapid demotion from cook. (You certainly don't want to find yourself confined to the galley amid all that congrealed grease in what is almost certainly the foulest area on the ship. Can there be anything else quite as disgusting as a marine dishcloth?)

Anyway, cooking is an impossible task — vital items such as can-opener, corkscrew, pliers, toilet paper will immediately go missing; and you'll be reduced to kneeling on the side-deck trying to open bottles by levering them on a cleat and tins by hammering your marline spike into them.

Far better to make your mark around the boat, coiling ropes and eagerly saying 'Aye aye, skipper'. No matter if you inadvertently let off the odd rocket flare and get the fire extinguisher going. ('Just testing her, skip.') Then, when they put on the winch, make sure you winch *with a will* — despite your unfortunate habit of pulling the rope round the drum *anti*-clockwise and of dropping the winch-handle overboard.

There's no need to feel guilty about this, though. *There's always one person on every boat who is just there to get in the way.* And the rest of the crew always enjoy watching someone make a mess of things, while they give one another those amused sidelong glances.

You might also try being seasick — even on a flat calm. This will buck up the morale of the rest of the crew no end and they'll tend to leave you even more alone — apart from carrying you between well and foredeck from time to time and forcing bracing tots between your lips.

Admittedly, as we've said, this 'last resort' approach may not do a great deal for your image. But by putting in a bit of hard work at the yacht club bar afterwards it shouldn't be too difficult to reestablish yourself (provided the rounds are on you). And having been well rested on board you may well find you have more energy to spare than your former crewmates to tell it like it wasn't.

○ ENCOUNTERS

The prospect of two boats colliding bears no relation to the amount of sea-room available.

The fact that power is supposed to give way to sail is no guarantee that it will

Whatever the rules may say, in a collision with a larger vessel, you lose

You may have seen the ferry, but it may not have seen you

If you think you've crossed clear ahead of the ferry, you may be wrong

On the occasions when you have right of way, the other vessel will be a supertanker

You never have right of way when you're up against a Mirror dinghy

12 The Club

**'Why don't you slip out of these wet clothes and into a
dry Martini?'**

Robert Benchley to Ginger Rogers in *The Major and the Minor*

As we said at the outset, it's on land that the Survival Sailor will really come into his own. And the first thing to do is to establish yourself in the yacht club. Admittedly, now that we can all get a piece of pontoon at a marina (at a price), a good many sailors feel it's no longer worth having to fork out for a yacht club tie (not to mention the dues), with the additional risk of getting

roped in to help organise the fitting-out party. But the yacht club is still where the *real* sailors are to be found, and no Survival Sailor can really afford *not* to belong to one.

The Survival Sailor, however, should be careful to choose a club that suits his style: a 'senior' club or a 'junior' club? One of the 'royals' (blazer and tie for dinner in the club restaurant)? Or a dinghy club or small inland sailing club on river, lake or puddle, (a leaky hut with no showers, a tea-urn for a bar, and bring your own sandwiches)? Do you want the sort of club where they break into sea-shanties or one where they break into rugby songs? Where they swap wives or swap stories? A club for 'winter sailors' (all fitting out and laying up), or for 'summer sailors' (where *some* members take to the water)? A club with a stronger 'racing section', or with a stronger 'cruising section'?

The choice, however, is not as great as it was. Some of the inland clubs have gone, with reservoirs in the Midlands and in the North running out of water. A fair number of dinghy clubs lost out to the sailing schools of the seventies. The bigger clubs are also up against it, and are now admitting power-boaters, waterskiers, fishermen, scuba-divers ('non-sailing members also welcome'). Whatever next? And even those long-established clubs with varnished boards listing flag officers since 1928 have had to bring in the slot machines, the pool tables, and the telly (for watching those America's Cup videos).

Some clubs, of course, probably wouldn't accept the Survival Sailor – like the New York Yacht Club or the Royal Yacht Squadron (which is said to have refused membership to a former prime minister not that long ago). You might make it into the RORC, though. Convince them you've done a bit of offshore racing and they'll usually take your money (to finance their burgeoning bureaucracy).

For the sake of his reputation, however, the Survival Sailor won't want a club that's *too* easy to join – the sort of place where you can just summon the steward and get him to sign you in. Any club worth its salt will have a proper waiting list rather than a box of membership applications forms inside the front door. And the better your club's reputation, the less trouble you are likely to encounter when you tie up at one of 'the royals' on one of your cruises and breeze into the bar saying: 'Don't mind if we clean up do you, steward – we're from the *Royal* Pudlington.' The fact is that facilities are still better at yacht clubs than in the marina portacabins. And there are those subsidised prices for booze and food (which will, at least, be *slightly* more palatable than it is on board).

The other advantage of belonging to a club is that it can be quite an agreeable way of boosting your credentials as a sailor – sitting on the terrace under that Martini parasol swapping stories with other club members about your epic voyages and pointing at all those duffers out on the water who don't know one end of a boat from the other.

The fact is that sailing clubs are about anything but sailing. The focus of activity is club politics, and sundry other activities – dinner-dances, marine auctions, photo-competitions, film shows, navigation lectures, sail-trimming classes, quiz nights, the summer ball, the AGM, fitting-out and laying-up parties, three-course Sunday lunches, the Christmas and New Year's Eve Party, Gala Nights, and the 'what were you wearing when the ship went down' fancy dress party.

All of this activity, of course – quite apart from organising the nautical side (joint cruises, club races, the protest committee) – does require a considerable hierarchy and committee network to keep it going. And since 'Who is Who' can be quite confusing at first, here's a guide to some of the principal positions and to some of the other club characters:

○ THE COMMODORE ○

The club chairman, whose term of office can last a number of years depending on the number of cocktail parties he throws. Despite his impressive nautical title, he need not have been a great racing helmsman. But he must have the means to steer the club through rough financial waters and to provide the odd trophy. *Perhaps, therefore, the ultimate position for the Survival Sailor who can afford it* – earning respect for the grandeur of his office rather than for his nautical abilities.

○ THE COMMODORE'S WIFE ○

May well have crewed for her husband at one time, but much prefers her current supportive role. This permits her to be the loudest woman in the club since she feels an obligation to liven things up socially, 'what with her husband being so tied up all the time with his business and his club responsibilities'. Not much liked by the other wives, however, despite all her efforts, continually shrieking away in a piercing Sloaney voice: 'Look at my

bottom – it's filthy' (referring to her Flying-Fifteen). Has two too many at the annual dinner-dance.

○ VICE-COMMODORE ○

The commodore-in-waiting. Of more immediate use than the commodore to the Survival Sailor, since the VC needs to be popular and, therefore, spends his money around the bar rather than on the club. Good man to cadge a drink, or two, off.

○ REAR-COMMODORE ○

The commodore very much in waiting – probably for a very long time. Not, therefore, someone the Survival Sailor need waste too much time buttering up, even though he is a flag officer of the club. And not a job for the Survival Sailor either since it often entails a good deal of organisational work.

○ SAILING SECRETARY RACE OFFICER ○

A type better avoided by the Survival Sailor. Expects to be bought drinks for organising 'a fine day's sport'. Though youngish, he is unlikely to defer to the

Survival Sailor's experience since he tends to know what he's talking about. When not officiating, he's racing – and often winning.

○ **CADET CAPTAIN** ○

An eighteen-year old version of the above who organises the kids (Cadets or Optimists). Often not actually all that good on the water, but unlike the race officer, this overgrown brat still has Olympic aspirations – fostered largely by his parents who 'believe in him' and who for the past fifteen years have been buying him a new Chèret sail, or whatever, whenever he loses (which is most of the time).

○ **CLUB SECRETARY** ○

The club bureaucrat, who also vets aspiring members. Thus, the person the Survival Sailor needs to bribe to get moved up the waiting list. Also the person who puts up all those notices:

'Dogs are not allowed on the premises.' (*But what about the Survival Sailor's parrot or pet panther?*)

'At no time should outside clothing i.e. caps, boots and oilskins be worn in either of the club bars.' (*Even for a Survival Sailor desperate to prove he's actually been out on the water?*)

'A member shall be answerable for the conduct of his guests while in the club.' (*Has he ever tried controlling the Survival Sailor's mates when they are three sheets in the wind?*)

'The anemometer must not be adjusted – thank you.' (*Even on a rainy day when there's nothing else to do?*)

○ SOCIAL SECRETARY ○

The woman who organises the regattas, bring-and-buys, second-hand gear sales, children's evenings, barn dances, barbecues, cheese and wine parties, discos, and is generally turned to for fund-raising solutions when the club is broke, i.e. most of the time. She will, in turn, turn to the Survival Sailor, among others. Be careful, though. These occasions are not usually a great success, and allowing yourself to get roped in will do little for your reputation. In fact, scorn is most likely to be the general reaction to your ingenious gala night menu of:

Between-The-Sheets Cocktail

*

Creme Fichyssoise

*

Nep-Tuna Salad

*

Cabin Sole

*

Rognons aux lumières de port

*

Banana Splice

○ THE BOSUN ○

Only found in larger clubs. Looks after the club boats and buoys, helps run the racing, and – important this, for the Survival Sailor – *rescue launches*. Often a character, with pipe and big sea boots, who spends his spare time splicing ropes with a marline spike, and striking a light with his Winners matches. Tends, however, to know a bit too much about wind and tides – what you'll come back and call a near-gale, he'll describe as some 'nice wee breeze'. If you keep him in baccy, though, he can be a good chap to scrounge tools off.

○ THE STEWARD ○

Often a hard-nosed ex-RN petty officer. Is paid a salary (if you can call it that) by the club, which may explain why he's so surly and unhelpful. He's the one who will accost the Survival Sailor and ask if he's a member when he tries to sneak into other clubs to use the showers. (In this event, the properly prepared Survival Sailor will have checked the name of the commodore and vice-commodore on the notice board at the entrance, flicked through the visitors book to see which members sign in the most guests, and, by dropping these names – as well as the name of the *Royal* Pudlington – should be able to get the steward himself to sign him in.)

○ THE BARMAN ○

Knows a Survival Sailor when he sees one. But provided you include him in every round you buy (NB: 'And one for yourself, Ron'; *NOT*: '*Another* one for yourself, Ron'), he can do you a bit of good – corroborating your stories ('Was that the time you broke your mast in the Fastnet, Mr Smith?') and giving your orders priority on crowded club nights. If you don't see him right, it'll tend to be the 'Who are you?' look when you walk in, rather than 'What'll it be, then, lads?' (And he may even tell you to take your wet wellies off before he serves you.)

○ THE RULES EXPERT ○

Probably a Survival Sailor heavily disguised. Is to be seen on the water very occasionally but has a suspiciously high rate of volunteering for the protest committee (thereby automatically disqualifying himself from racing). Does know the rules though (he's very often a solicitor) – insofar as the rules of sailing and racing are knowable. Gives long boring talks on obscure paragraphs on winter evenings, which, unfortunately for any Survival Sailor in his vicinity, he will continue at the bar: 'It's not commonly known that Rule 8(2) IYRU 1985-88 allows one to moor on the starting line, but what if your anchor-warp's over?'

○ THE PRO ○

A club member who sails for a living – delivering boats, instructing, offshore racing. Despite his vivid accounts of great wealth (and women) made as paid skipper of luxury yachts in the Caribbean, he is often rather hard up 'between jobs'. Is, therefore, prepared to keep company with and boost the reputation of a Survival Sailor who keeps his Seagrams topped up. Can also be a bit of a bore, though, with his 'rorky' tales of how he 'shinned up the mast to cut away the twisted kite at the Sunk in last year's North Sea Race', and about his 'frequent' encounters with 'Harry' (Cudmore) and 'old DC' (Conner).

Although a Survival Sailor can have a fine onshore sailing career as a prominent member of the club, it is not absolutely necessary to occupy any of these official positions. It is not too difficult to find another excuse for not being seen on the water very often.

In fact, it's often sufficient just to spend enough time hanging around the club to be 'excused boats'. The important thing is to be seen as someone who really *belongs*. This will mean doing your bit to make the bar a going concern (in view of the precarious financial situation of most sailing clubs). This will not usually prove too onerous a chore for the Survival Sailor, who should be as ready as the next man to hold forth, pint in hand, about what 12-metre racing was like BC (Before Conner), and what it will be like AD (After Dennis). You also will be expected to corroborate the stories of duels with the deep of all the other Survival Sailors at the club – just as they will corroborate yours. (Yarn-spinning, of course, is one of the traditional activities of sailing folk.)

It looks good, too, if you carry yourself like a sailor. They do say you can tell a seafaring man by the way he moves around the boat. Well, you can also tell one by the way he moves around the bar. So tread gently when you leave your stool. A brothel-creeping shuffle is the sort of thing, perhaps giving the occasional lurch before steadying yourself on the bar. (This comes fairly naturally to most Survival Sailors.) And for that final touch of authenticity, it's worth limping into the bar, looking crestfallen, at least once or twice a year, clutching a broken tiller in your hand.

○ ANCHORING

A sheltered place to anchor will remain so only until you get your anchor down

If the anchor comes adrift, it will be between 3 and 4 in the morning

Everyone will arrive back at the harbour at the same time

It's harder to get back in than it was to get out

The anchor warp always drags

It's an even bigger drag to fix it

When you think you won't need a second anchor, you will

13 Walking the Dock

'When you got it, flaunt it!'

Zero Mostel

More and more this is what après sail is all about, and where the Survival Sailor *must* distinguish himself. Although the phrase 'walking the dock' has only recently reached this side of the Atlantic, the phenomenon is already well established. Basically it means seeing and being seen around the yacht club or marina, at the *right* time, wearing the *right* clothes, and saying and doing the *right* things – preferably on the *right* boat.

There is no standard itinerary. This generally will depend on the layout of your particular dock. It may be a circuit (clockwise or anti-clockwise); or a straight back-and-forth stretch of pier; or it may all take place in a more concentrated milling-around zone.

When laying a course round the dock, though, the Survival Sailor should try to take in all the spots where he or she will be seen at best advantage (whether shopping, posing, or adjusting gear). Try to avoid those areas where the tourists congregate. Don't, however, omit that vantage point to be found on every dock or marina which provides the best view of folk making a mess of getting their sails up and down, and giving you and your fellow dockwalkers the occasion to comment on other people's mooring techniques. There will also, of course, be the cock-up of the day to talk about (try to make sure it isn't *yours*).

There is no particular time for walking the dock. But, as with the summer evening walkabout in any Mediterranean town, it does tend to take place mainly after 6 pm. Some Survival Sailors, however, manage to cut a rather fine figure by doing their rounds in the early morning. Making plenty of noise to wake up the other boats, they trundle along their trolleys (fully loaded with picnic cooler and the sail-bags of the most expensive sailmakers – even if they don't have the sails to go with them), looking as if they're about to embark on a major expedition. Having made their point, they can then motor off round the headland in search of some secluded estuary where they can lie low and booze for a day or two.

Alternatively, you can simply take up a position on one of the main dockwalking routes and conspicuously busy yourself varnishing a piece of wood for the old boat you are restoring while offering knowledgeable comments about the weather to those getting ready for sea, and generally making those people who are still staggering around in their pyjamas feel thoroughly ashamed of themselves.

For this 'early bird' routine to really come off, though, the impression should be conveyed that you *have already been out on the water* (and are thus under no obligation to go out again). It's important, therefore, to have that 'damp look', rather than the 'crumpled look' of someone who has just spent the night aboard sleeping in his clothes. Ideally, you'll have your wet sails up to dry.

You will, of course, make it clear from your meteorological remarks that you are speaking *from experience*. So when someone (perhaps another Survival Sailor) says doubtfully, 'looks as if it's blowing up', you can reply heartily: 'Nonsense – great sailing wind.' If they claim it must be a Force 6 out there, you can reply, *with authority*: 'You must be joking – Force 4 at the most.'

As a general rule, however, it is in the evening that the Survival Sailor and the other dockwalkers will be seen in action in their finest livery, hailing one another, spinning their yarns, and looking over the boats, *and each other*.

To the casual observer, of course, it may seem as if nothing very much is going on. By no means everyone who is strolling around the dock is actually walking the dock. The trippers who wander about offering the odd comment of 'Nice yacht, mister', will be completely unaware of the drama that is being played out around them. Not that the insiders will ever *admit* that what they are doing is 'walking the dock'. They're simply 'winding down' after a hard day on the water. In practice, though, they will know *exactly* what is going on, and so must the Survival Sailor. So let's go step by step through this exercise in 'sea and be seen'.

○ THE WALK ○

As we've seen, walking the dock is a good deal more than a mere walk round the dock. But, as at the bar, it is important to get the walk itself right. Rule number one is *don't hurry*. Even if you are desperate to get to a proper loo after ten days at sea, *never run on the dock*. On the other hand, don't be too casual about it: it is possible to walk *off* a dock, or to step into a puddle of lubricating oil or fresh diesel.

Essentially, the walk is a saunter or a stroll, with feet perhaps a little splayed, ready to shuffle around in half-circles whenever you decide to dally. In fact, you tend to move in a sort of zig-zag round the dock constantly shifting your direction as you stop to check someone's rigging or to greet a fellow yachtsman. The zig-zag also helps you to keep your speed in check. Not only should you never hurry on the dock, *you shouldn't overtake on the dock.* (This can irritate your fellow sailors as much as if you were overhauling them at sea.) At times, though, it will be necessary to speed up, such as when approaching the pub, so as to establish an overlap on other dockwalkers before you reach the door of the saloon bar.

It is not a good idea, however, to overdo the walk with too heavy a nautical roll or list, as if you have difficulty keeping your feet on terra firma. This really requires you to sport a pipe, peg-leg, parrot, penny-whistle and all the other old sea-dog paraphernalia – which is a bit passé these days. The Survival Sailor will be much better off with a sort of nimble shuffle, weight on the balls of the feet, constantly poised, panther-like, to spring into action – much as he might be on the boat (or at the bar).

The walk can be adapted, of course, according to the sort of sailor you are (or claim to be). The 'rorky' will tend to have shoulders forward, waist in, weight into the wind. The cruising man will have a more sedate stay-awhile gait. With the dinghy sailor you probably won't even notice the walk – he'll be so loaded down with equipment – trapeze harness, sailbags, the latest copy of *Yachts and Yachting* etc.

But if dinghies are your thing, or one of the other more athletic forms of sailing, it may be worth building a few callisthenics into your walk – perhaps a bit of arm-flexing, getting those trapezoids working. Once again, though, do be sure to pick a spot where you are in full view – perhaps at the top of the main gangway at low tide.

○ THE LOOK ○

Just as sailors don't like to be overtaken at sea, so they don't like to be overtaken in matters of dress. As we've seen, even the average cruising family tends to be kitted out like offshore racers these days. Usually, therefore, the gear will be top of the range (Musto rather than Marks and Spencer) – though some attempt should be made to match it to the kind of boat that you sail.

Attention to detail is vital. You must make sure you are wearing the 'in' shade of deck shoes and that you have the right logo on your t-shirt. Do make sure, too, that you know what the gear represents before you wear it on the dock. If you wear white dungarees, for instance, you'll probably be taken for the paid steward from a rich man's yacht.

But 'the look' on the dock is not all about clothes. It's also a question of being seen *doing* the right thing. Dockwalkers like to perpetuate the illusion that this is actually a busy time of day – not simply an exercise in swanning about. For the Survival Sailor, the thing to remember is – whatever you do, *do it right.* You may not be doing very much – suntanning, coiling a rope, inspecting your boat. But better this than looking lubberly by attempting something too advanced – like stripping down a winch or going up the mast in a bosun's chair to sort out the halyards.

A good choice is folding (and unfolding) your sails concertina fashion ('flaking them down' as the Survival Sailor will call it just to show he knows his stuff); or hoisting your spinnaker to dry. Once again, however, don't be in too much of a rush to get the sails stowed. For although walking the dock is basically about getting ready for the cocktail hour, the impression should be given that your main concern is getting your boat shipshape for your next voyage.

○ THE SOCIAL ROUND ○

This is usually the final phase of walking the dock and can take place either on board, in the club bar, or at the pub. If it is the pub, though, it should, of course, be the *right* pub for you (whether it be the cruising pub, the racing pub, the old salts' pub, or the trendy pub).

The socially ambitious Survival Sailor, however, will normally aim to sip his cocktails on board one of the swishier yachts (rather than round the dinette from a plastic mug). The essence of dockwalking, after all, is the ancient sport of snobbery.

Thus, it's important that the Survival Sailor's route round the dock always takes in the *right* pontoon, usually where the Nicholsons and Swans are moored. After a while he should become an accepted figure on that pontoon. The Survival Sailor will know he's arrived when not only do the top people respond when he hails them, *but when they, unprompted, hail him.* If all he gets is an uncomprehending stare when he offers his greetings, he'd probably better find somewhere else to do his hailing.

Establishing yourself in the right company won't be easy, of course, if all you own is one of the standard production-line craft. In this case it may hardly seem worth the outlay in bribes to the harbour master to get yourself a berth on the right pontoon.

Probably a better bet, therefore, is to charter some exotic vessel for a few weekends, throw a few parties for the folk from the right pontoon, and then spend the rest of your Survival Sailing career getting invited back (or inviting yourself back). If asked about your exotic vessel, you can always say you are now keeping her permanently moored in the Mediterranean.

⦿ THE CHAT ⦿

The talk, of course, whether you're in the pub or clinking glasses in the cockpit will inevitably be nautical. The Survival Sailor, therefore, should make a point of studying the sailing magazines carefully to make sure he's up to date with all the latest technological refinements, like 'gennakers' and all those moveable parts under the keel that have come in post-Perth.

It's probably better not to overdo the nautical yarns any more than it is to go in for too much of the 'Aye aye, me hearties' or 'Avast abaft' when you greet people on the dock. (This doesn't really go with the sort of gear the Survival Sailor will probably be sporting.)

Far better to make your mark with a few telling technical observations: about Kevlar the wonder-fibre, for example ('But will it last, I ask you?'). No harm either in coining a few hi-tech terms of your own as you discuss sail area or VMG. (Never call it 'Velocity Made Good'.)

Do take care, though, that your basic ignorance doesn't show through the jargon – calling them 'yachts' instead of boats for instance; or saying rope when you can say cordage; or by asking someone why his sails are so dirty (after he's spent ten times over the odds on special khaki hi-tech, low-stretch fibre).

The Survival Sailor should, however, make a point of never sounding too overawed by the latest developments in gear or boats. Thus, the Survival Sailor's comment on the craft that everyone on the dock has been admiring is more likely to be along the lines of: 'Not another David Thomas job. Isn't it about time this country produced some other offshore racing boat designers?'

A good chance to show off your technical knowledge will be at the chandler's shop (one of your habitual ports of call when walking the dock).

Even if you're a mere cruising man, make a point of getting involved in a lengthy discussion on the merits of the LCD mini-radar system or the latest light-weight Lewmar self-tailing winch. Once again, a certain scepticism is important. Never seem totally convinced when the chandler reassures you about the breaking strain of Kevlar core: 'No stretch in the vertical plane you say – but what worries me is that it may break down in the horizontal.' The chandler (and the onlookers) should be left in no doubt that the Survival Sailor's style is hard to windward rather than never sailing with the wind forward of the beam.

○ BOAT JIBES ○

Above all, though, dockside chat will tend to be about the boats themselves – with the emphasis on slightly snide remarks about other boats moored in the vicinity.

It is, however, less important for the Survival Sailor to know how the boats sail than how they rate in the social pecking order. Thus you will be able to adapt your remarks as appropriate and 'fit in' when invited aboard.

When moored next to a Swan, for instance, your comment to the owner as he emerges from his large blue Mercedes might be: 'Those Finns certainly make lovely boats – but don't you feel a bit guilty about not buying British?'

No need, however, to let patriotism inhibit you from quaffing his Mumm champagne (they say you know you're following a Swan by the trail of Champagne corks), while you leaf through his back numbers of *Boat International*. Whether or not you then go on to point out some of the design faults of this particular model will depend on how much you want to get invited back.

Down, the social scale a bit, you find the Swans of the British boat industry – the Oysters and Nicholsons. But though Oysters may be good enough for Clare Francis and the Admiral of the RORC, there's no harm in the Survival Sailor expressing certain reservations: 'Excellent RORC boat no doubt. But just how quick is it round the buoys?'

As always, however, the Survival Sailor will know the form on board. A gin and tonic is the drink to ask for and *Yachting World* the mag to refer to. And since racing is important to the owner (plenty of heavy weather gear in evidence), you'll make the right impression if you're clad in Musto, Equinoxe or Helly-Hansen, and perhaps drive a Jag (not, however, the latest registered letter).

Racing features have also been built into a great many of the other boats in the marina of the eighties – much as their owners will protest that they sail *to relax*. Hence the popularity of the fast cruising boats like the Sadler, Moody, Bénéteau and Jeanneau. So, although you'll find their owners sociable enough (usually a bottle of vino or perhaps a quick six-pack if they're anxious to push on), this may well conceal a mean competitive streak. The Survival Sailor would do well to be a bit wary, therefore, when he steps aboard – especially if that ad is anything to go by: 'Invite them for dinner, then eat them for breakfast.'

If this prospect doesn't worry you, an appropriate put-down for a Sadler owner would be some remark about that boat industry soap opera, 'Howards Way', in which Sadler boats have starred. The Bénéteau you might dismiss as one of those Continental production-line jobs without any real pedigree: 'Just think, only a few years ago a moribund fishing boat manufacturer on the French Atlantic coast – and today the busiest assembly line of them all. Sharp businesswoman that Madame Roux.'

With French-made boats, you might also venture the odd suggestion that *the owner may have gone over to the other side.* (Anglo-French rivalry runs as deep in yachting as in most other things.)

You may find, though, that this is like water off a frog's back – so committed are these people to their Citroen CX, and to reading *Voiles et Voiliers* instead of *Yachting Monthly*, secure in their Club Med vision of the world. (In the ads these boats are always pictured in transparently blue water with transparently clad wenches soaking up the sun at precisely the spot where most other boats have winches.)

Hardly surprising, therefore, that it's in this group of boats that you often find some of the fiercest exchanges (particularly when they are moored alongside one another). Thus, perhaps, Sadler to Bénéteau (pretending not to notice the Red Ensign clearly flying on the stern): 'Bonjour, capitaine, vous étes d'ou en France exactement?' Or Bénéteau to Sadler (when the latter are tucking into a Chinese takeaway): 'I say, squire, don't happen to have any pure olive oil on board do you – run out and we're having salade niçoise ce soir'.

The Survival Sailor, however, should always keep his jibes within bounds – going just far enough to show he knows his boats; but not so far that he is invited to sign the visitor's book and push off. It's not always easy, though, to know *how far* you can go. Sometimes even the most innocent remark can be taken as a deadly insult.

Aboard a Westerly, for instance, you can normally count on a warm welcome with a mug of tea and buttered scones and an intelligent chat about the latest issue of *Practical Boat Owner*. But any mention of the phrase 'floating caravan' (in whatever context) will probably mean that's the last time you will be allowed to darken your host's gangway.

By contrast, the Westerly owner will probably welcome some criticism of the adjustment of his racing rigging. (Even Westerly folk seem to be getting caught up in the 'go-faster syndrome'. As the copywriters put it: 'There's a Westerly rising – it's going to be a storm!')

○ MISHAPS

There is no such thing as plain sailing

Anything can happen on a boat, and it usually does

No instruction manual will cater for the situations *you* will get into

Someone *was* watching when you goofed

If a sail-bag can roll off the deck, it will

Your winch-handle is more likely to fall overboard if you don't have a spare

The mast will always fall to leeward – except when you're standing to windward

If a halyard jams, it will always be when you need to get your sail down immediately

---

14 Looking the Part

'Odd's fish, Sir Percy, you're brainless, spineless and useless, but you do know clothes'

The Scarlet Pimpernel

As you will by now have gathered, looking the part is at least as important to the Survival Sailor as knowing how to sail the boat. But the really skilled Survival Sailor should be able to look *quite a number of parts*. Each type of sailing has its own distinct look. And since the Survival Sailor is someone who gets around the sailing scene and who doesn't like to be pinned down too easily, he will find it often pays off *not* to conform to the company he is keeping at any particular time (with all the attendant risks of exposing his ignorance). He may prefer instead to turn out in the style of one of the *other* sailing groups.

Thus among the cruising fraternity, you may find the Survival Sailor sporting full IOR emblazoned rugby shirt, white shorts, and *brown* worn-without-socks 'Sebago Docksides' (*not* those brightly coloured shoes which turn your toes red, green or yellow), and telling the assembled company: 'Wish I had the time to drift about like you chaps, but, you know, it's the Admirals' Cup again next year and ....'.

Should he find himself among the racing gang, or at least among people who pretend to be 'rorkies', the Survival Sailor will appear suitably bronzed in his bolero wetsuit. ('Give me dinghy racing any day. You can keep your paid professionals and £100,000 boats that are out of date before they're built.')

When posing as a hard dinghy racer, you can often simply let your t-shirt do your talking for you. T-shirts really come into their own in this group. But do make sure it carries the right sort of message i.e. 'FD Worlds, Malmo, Sweden 1980' or 'Copa del Rey, Palma de Mallorca 1986' rather than 'Pudlington Cadet Gala'.

It's vitally important, of course, to get the look accurate. Sailors do rather pride themselves on being able to judge a man 'by the cut of his jib'. And while the Survival Sailor may go astray at sea, he can't afford to give himself away with his turnout. Here, then, is a rough guide to some of the styles you might care to adopt:

○ **WINDSURFER** ○

Physique permitting, as little as possible should be worn, apart from the tan. Those brightly coloured cotton 'board shorts' that shrink onto the thighs are normally the order of the day in the Med. In more northern climes, try a 'shortie' wetsuit and perhaps a pair of neoprene mittens and 'Okewind' non-slip boots. Any other clothing should be brightly coloured in pastel shades of pink, blue or grey (this year anyway). Accessories might include the little plastic drum on a draw cord round your neck (for carrying your valuables); and a harness/life-vest casually draped over your shoulder can come in useful for concealing a pot belly. If you're down south, don't forget the splash of silver factor 15 sun block on the bridge of the nose. It may also be worth bleaching your hair (if you're under thirty). When renting a car, a beach buggy or Land Rover are ideal. A Golf GTI would also do the job (if suitably clapped out) – but *not* a Ford Escort. In fact, the windsurfing vehicle, par excellence, is the battered tenth-hand Dormobile (appropriately decorated with sailmakers' stickers and surfing graffiti) which also serves as a club-house.

○ FAMILY ○

To come over as a 'family' sailor, a Ford Escort would be just the thing, or perhaps an Austin Metro. ('Really like something a bit bigger, but can't afford it what with the boat and the kids.')

When it comes to clobber, whether for cruising or dinghy, the family sailor tends to 'dress down' of necessity – if only to set an example to his offspring who keep clamouring for the latest offshore racing gear. A pair of old khaki shorts and any old heavy-duty jumper would have done at one time, but now it's more likely to be jeans and a fisherman's knit or cable-knit sweater (made by the wife). Accessories might include the lockspike knife on a lanyard round the neck, spare shackles jangling in pockets, and perhaps a baby's rattle ('Wish I had more time on the water, but you know, young family and all that'). Don't bother with a belt, though – a piece of Marlow 5 mm pre-stretch rope will do nicely ('You never know when you may need it').

Some Survival Sailors rather shy away from the 'family' sailing look, but it can come in very useful in an emergency – such as when playing on a harbour master's or a lock-keeper's sympathies ('I'll pay you on the way back if that's all right – you know how it is').

○ CRUISING ○

Much more gear-conscious today, as we have seen. The rust brown sailcloth trousers and the heavy grey or navy sweater decorated with polyurethane varnish are long gone. Now, with the arrival of the more swishily appointed boats, the cruising man is altogether more chic in brightly coloured wellies, white roll-neck, tailored reefer jacket and designer jeans, with even the odd pair of white shorts making an appearance (though these tend to be more 'Med' and 'IOR'). There'll be the usual junk in the pockets – split pins, stud links, spiles, snap hooks, but these days he's more likely to be carrying Phillips and electricians' screwdrivers ('Really – the electrics on these modern boats'), rather than the rusty paint-stained multipurpose ¼-inch-bladed prodder of yesteryear.

◯ **IOR** ◯

Very distinctive gear, though the IOR look has had an impact on almost all other sailing groups. It should, of course, be worn with the cock-of-the-walk swagger of people who believe they dominate the sport. On the water it'll probably be Helly-Hansen Admiral's Cup suit, Musto 3-level Ocean Wear, or the even more chic French Gul or Equinoxe outfits (all, of course, with built-in flotation and rescue light, and breaking all records for the number of Velcro-fixed pockets).

The above are usually his or her *own* gear worn while racing as an amateur (i.e. practising). When racing as a professional (i.e. racing), it'll be a coloured-coordinated uniform of a similar type supplied by the boat's sponsor or by its wealthy skipper/owner.

What you wear onshore will depend on whether you are gentlemen (i.e. rich owner/skipper) who can wear his usual clothes (blazer, DAKS trousers, Paul and Shark turtle-neck sweater etc), or player. The latter – the young blond hulks who grind the winches and trim the sails on these water-borne rocket ships – will still be wearing team colours. These include the rugby-style racing shirt (designed and made by Ocean World, Cowes) in the same shade as the boat's hull, with the emblem of the boat (normally the same as its battle-flag) decorating the left breast. White shorts are *de rigueur*, along with Javelin 'warmer' coat or Puffa jacket.

The Survival Sailor should be careful not to be let down by his spouse/girlfriend. (IOR folk are always accompanied by an admiring coterie – usually female.) Thus wife/mistress of gentleman IOR should be seen all Gucci and Pucci, and Céline shoes, ordering her handmade Louis Vuitton luggage to be loaded out of her white Porsche 928S. (Could come a bit expensive for the Survival Sailor, this.) The players' girls will be equally, but less expensively, decorative – filling out their jeans and t-shirts in the right sort of places, with deep-water tans and bleached hair that match their menfolk's.

○ **LONG-DISTANCE RACING** ○

Round-the-world sailors tend to be recognisable as much by their physiognomy as by their gear: hollow bloodshot eyes (from the salt-spray and all those sleepless nights); tanned, wind-whipped faces (but marble-white from the neck down as a result of never getting out of their ocean suits for weeks or months at a time); spotty complexion (from using 'wipes' or sea-water to wash in); weals on the hands and forearms (from getting careless with those coffee-grinder winches).

They also tend to be prone to abrupt changes of mood, with their body-clocks having been programmed to four hours on/four hours off for so long. Their senses may also be dulled by exposure to cabin stench, stale sweat, continual damp and weeks of running downwind at fifteen knots in the Southern Ocean. Disorientation on land may also be common, with that characteristic staggering walk of people who have spent too long at sea.

Not a bad role for the Survival Sailor, though – if you are handy enough with the make-up to get the look right. The single gold earring is also a nice touch – for the boys at least. (After all, it's not that far from living the life of a pirate, and pop-stars do it.)

You will then only be required to put in the most occasional of appearances on the dock. (These Whitbread types often find it hard to adjust on land and usually can't wait to get back to another long haul and blow a few more thousand pounds worth of spinnakers: 'After all, what else is there?')

Needless to say, the Survival Sailor shouldn't be seen to ring the changes in gear too often at his local yacht club. People might begin to get a tiny bit suspicious. But, as we've seen, he or she is a versatile performer and does like to get around. Be careful, though, *where* you wear your different outfits: the IOR ploy may do wonders for your reputation on one of your visits to Little Pudlington YC, but it could prove your undoing at a rorky drinks party during Cowes week.

○ TENDERS

An inflatable always moves away faster than someone swimming towards it

No inflatable can be inflated in the time stated in the manufacturer's instructions

Most tenders are equipped with only one functioning rowlock

If you want to go to the pub and there's only one tender and too many people, you will all try to get into that tender

If your tender is not securely moored, it may not be moored at all when you get back

If you want to know if it rained the previous night, look in the dinghy

Show a child how to operate an outboard motor, and he will

15 Racing

**'I roar down to the grinders, "Spit blood! Spit blood!
This is what you were born for!"'**

John Bertrand, *Born to Win*

For the Survival Racer, there is really only one Racing Rule – *don't*. A rash attempt to dash round the buoys to give credence to some of your club bar claims, can all too easily wreck a carefully crafted reputation.

The fact is, however, that we all enjoy seeing our boat go faster than someone else's, and the thought of seeing our boat go faster than *everyone* else's can be tempting. Survival Racers should know better, but, perhaps fired by watching one of those America's Cup videos, they have been known to throw caution to the winds and opt for a 'Life on the wire' (well, a couple of hours anyway), in the company of all those other nuts who keep the osteopaths in business.

All very unwise – especially when the savvy Survival Racer can so easily become part of the 'racing scene' without having to actually take part in a race. It's not too difficult to mug up on the rules and to become a stalwart of the protest committee. (The only danger here is that it might make you a few enemies at the club – racers who lose their protests *never* forget.)

A better option perhaps, for the Survival Racer who is also an aspiring club official, is to 'serve' on the committee boat. You can thus spend the race getting quietly smashed whilst commenting authoritatively on all the tactical blunders the fleet leaders are making out on the water, and reminiscing about your own racing days when you used to use a sort of 'scalloping' technique to windward long before Conner ever got round to it. The reason *you* are not out there is that you're more of a distance racer – 'nothing much shorter than 150 miles'. And you'll have had your toughies, as you'll let the rest of the committee know. There was that Force 9 on the Cowes/St Malo one year when you led the fleet with three reefs and the storm jib all the way. Not that things always worked out. There was that time your helmsman lost his concentration: 'Electrics burnt out, fracture in the mast, crew feeding on dry bread like a flock of gannets on the weather rail, *and* we were taking in water. With a sixty-two-knot wind across the deck, not much choice but to pack it in.' Still, that was nothing to the time when there were twenty broken masts before you got out of the Solent . . .

Another perfectly sound cop-out, though rather less fun, is to volunteer to help the ladies to get the lunch: 'I really don't see why in this day and age the women should be expected to do all this work on their own.'

Once you've found yourself a niche on the sidelines though, make sure you hang in there. Do not, in a weak moment, succumb to pressure to enter the regatta 'just to make up the numbers'. But be diplomatic about it. A straightforward refusal may seem a bit unsporting on the part of someone who has spent so much time at the club bar explaining his 'peeling' technique and holding forth so knowledgeably on the finer points of that fateful last downwind leg of the 1983 America's Cup. Your best bet here is one of those standard health ploys – perhaps the old bad back: 'Doctor's orders, I'm afraid. First came on when I started wearing weights for Laser racing. And those three hours strung out on a trapeze a day or so ago seems to have put me out of action for quite some while.' This can sound even better coming from the wife: 'Charles would just love to race, but his chiropracter, you know . . .'

Alternatively, if you can pull it off, and have managed to establish your credentials as a long-distance racer, you simply laugh off the invitation to participate in the regatta, making no secret of your contempt for people who go round the buoys for a couple of hours and call it a day's sailing.

Another way out (of offshore) is to wait until the race itself and then get drummed out by the safety officer: 'Fussy bastard scratched me because I didn't have a spare winch-handle.' (If the safety officer doesn't notice, or misses you out on his 'random check', you'll simply have to call out to him: 'I don't need a spare winch-handle, do I, squire?')

But as we said at the outset, not all Survival Racers will want to take the easy way out. You may have just invested in a new boat which, according to the propaganda, could sail itself round the course; or you may still be smarting from those family taunts that all you know about sailing could be written on the back of a postage stamp. Whatever the reason, the sad fact is that many Survival Racers just won't be deterred from their bid for greater glory than they have so far earned in the yacht club bar.

Fortunately, however, a number of stratagems have been developed to help the Survival Racer. These won't always ensure that you romp home with flying colours. But, with any luck, they should enable you to cross the line flying your protest flag (like everyone else). And you should at least stand a good chance of finishing in the top half of the field – provided, that is, that half of the boats pull out after the first leg.

○ PICKING YOUR RACE ○

If you are determined to race, make sure it's the right one. Careful race selection should be a vital part of the Survival Racer's strategy. As a general rule, you should only enter a race where you can put into effect one of the plans outlined later in this chapter.

Like other competitors (but for different reasons), you'll also need to examine very carefully the shape of the coastline, where the buoys or marks will be placed, how long the race will last, probable wind and weather conditions. The programme may say 'Racing Instructions – Standard'. But there's nothing standard about most races – particularly the way the Survival Racer goes about it (as we shall see).

As often as not, the Survival Racer will be advised to pick a race where the standard is likely to be low, or perhaps where there are only four starters: thus, in the latter case, by putting only one boat out of action you can be sure to finish at least third. (That isn't to say that the Survival Racer can't come out ahead even if there's a very strong field – see Plan 1 below.)

Another good choice is often the Handicap race – if you've managed to get your fishing smack admitted (see Plan 2). With any luck you should be able to start with the advantage of an enormous handicap, provided you've successfully flummoxed the 'measurer' who rated you. You won't be relying purely on your handicap, of course. Your clanking rust-bucket will make such a racket that you should be able to motor for most of the race without anyone noticing. Make sure incidentally that she has a name like 'Buoy-Basher' or 'Rammer' – this should be rather more effective than a name like 'Sleepytime Gal' in persuading the opposition to give you a wide berth.

Another advantage of a handicap race is that if things go wrong, you always can claim you just entered for 'a bit of fun'. Anyway, the results won't be known for days afterwards – especially with the amount of time it'll take the committee to work out how to assess 'Rammer's' performance. This also gives you time to think up a few good excuses.

Finally, for the Survival Racer who is still looking for a respectable cop-out, there is always the 'non-race'. This entails very careful study of the weather reports, and then turning up ready and raring to race on a morning with a Force 12 blowing when clearly there's no way that a race can take place. (You'd better make sure, of course, that you haven't got some madman as race organiser.) Then you can spend the morning in the club bar, strolling over to the noticeboard from time to time to stare wistfully at the rear commodore's communication: 'Race No 4 has been abandoned by the committee and will be sailed on a date to be announced later.' Such a pity that the new date to be set won't prove possible for you.

○ **PREPARATION** ○

Do check that you've got enough insurance cover. There may be something in the small print which means they won't pay out if they can claim it was your fault, i.e. like that port-starboard collision last time you raced when you tried to fall off behind the other boat but forgot to ease the mainsheet. So make sure you can afford to smash your boat up. It's also worth checking what liability you might have for damage to your crew — someone's bound to get their head dented by the boom or their hand crushed in a winch.

With any luck, of course, the rights and wrongs of any incident that may occur will be sorted out in *your* favour. But the Survival Sailor shouldn't just trust to luck. Try to see to it that you have at least one staunch ally on the protest committee. And make a point of getting your 'witnesses' lined up in advance. If you're using Plan 3, you'll need at least four people on shore who are prepared to swear blind that they saw you through their binoculars go round *each* buoy *twice*.

It can also pay to work in collusion with the crew of another boat who will be prepared to commit multiple perjury in confirming later that you made *every* effort to avoid the incident, and that the reason you gybed so suddenly was to avoid a passing whale. (You and your crew will do the same for them, of course, on another occasion.)

You needn't have too bad a conscience about this sort of approach. After all, everyone else in the race will sign off afterwards to confirm that they competed 'in a sportsmanlike manner'. They'll go to their graves *claiming* that they never touched the mark. Not that this should come as any surprise. All racers know it's 'kill or be killed' at the leeward mark. It's a good job the committee boat has no idea what goes on out there. They'd be quite shocked. (Well, perhaps.)

The fact is that the rules are there to be broken. Remember that rule which says that when you know you've infringed a rule, you are supposed to retire? This surely was never intended to be taken seriously. (It is, however, a rule the Survival Racer might well bear in mind. Not only could it offer an easy way out; it could also add to your reputation as an officer and a gentleman.)

○ THE CREW ○

Choice of crew, of course, will depend on the vessel you're racing. But in most cases, assuming the Survival Racer opts, as he often will, for one of the larger craft (say a half-tonner), the following should be part of your team:

Strongman. Has a vital role to play in all those close-quarter situations. The rules may say that 'yachts shall not make contact in the course of a race'. But, as we all know, racing is a 'contact sport'. So ideally, you need someone who is a dab hand with a boathook (should the occasion arise to hole your closest rival below the waterline). Long arms are also a help for grabbing the opposition's boom if it swings your way, and also for hauling your boat round the buoy (when no one's looking).

Midget. Your 'extra' man or woman. No need to penalise yourself, of course, by *admitting* to this additional crew member (who can usually be smuggled aboard in a sail-bag). The Survival Racer, however, needs all the hands he can get. The midget will act mainly as a lookout to warn of upcoming situations (i.e. if there's a boat stealing up on you that might hear your motor; or when you might do well to confuse the enemy by short-tacking). Can also be useful for foredeck work under the genoa foot.

Close Relative(s) of the Commodore. Another vital member of the team who really comes into his/her own when you're up before the protest committee. (Make sure that for any race you enter there are at least two very close friends of the Commodore on the protest committee.)

Hailer. Perhaps the key position (apart from your own as skipper and tactician). Leads the attack in those verbal duels you'll be having with other boats for most of the race. His fiendish yell when you luff could make all the difference. But it's not enough just to intimidate a right-of-way boat. He needs to sound *convincing* when he shouts 'No water', 'Distance from the buoy', 'Sailing above your proper course'; or when he yells 'starboard' (when you're in fact on port) just to confuse the opposition; or calls for room to tack when you don't actually need it.

He must also have a voice that *carries*: when you're about 100 yards behind a boat that's about to round the mark, his yell of 'waatah, waatah at the mark' should sound as if you're right on their stern, thus distracting them for long enough for you to get to their stern, scream 'Overlap' and slip inside them. Same with his 'Mast abeam' – it should give you time to actually get his mast abeam.

One quality you might look for in selecting your crew is a pronounced suicidal streak. You may well need people who will be prepared to live (or die) with some of your more 'adventurous' tactics. Say, for instance, things are looking desperate at the last weather mark and you are trailing the fleet home on the final run. After rounding the mark, an extra dose of speed will now be vital. So, you may have no choice but to get the crew to hoist all downwind sails – large spinnaker, blooper, big boy, staysail, and then very coolly announce: 'OK, chaps, over the side with the lot of you – I'll stay on here and try to save the day. Don't worry – this is what they used to do in the Sydney Harbour eighteen-footers. Worked every time, fantastic extra speed without your weight. Be back for you all later!'

○ SETTING UP YOUR BOAT ○

You may be racing your old fishing smack, or your converted lifeboat. Or you may be racing your new super-boat, with all the latest gear, top sails and 'go-fast' gadgetry – if only to make up for your lack of sailing skill. But whichever it is, do make sure that her topsides are well armoured. Those boat-to-boat confrontations are hard to avoid in racing – and there's no sense in getting your crew's legs crushed fending off other boats. On occasion, too, of course, you may decide to ram. *And when a Survival Racer rams, he rams hard.* If he also has right-of-way, he rams *very, very* hard.

That isn't to say, of course, that the Survival Racer is oblivious to the finer points, such as blanketing a boat to leeward, or performing the odd 'slam-drunk' covering tack so beloved of the 12-metre boys. It's simply that he sometimes finds other methods more effective.

With this in mind, make sure you have everything on board that you may need: that length of cable that the strongman can use to haul you round the mark; and those small buckets (tied to pieces of rope with snap shackles on the end) – which the strongman will try to slip on to the transom of other boats in those tight situations.

Don't, of course, forget your protest flag, which you should have at the ready even as you get under way. You'll probably have to start flashing it as soon as the five-minute gun goes, and then keep on flashing it all the way, not forgetting to show it to the committee boat when you come in. (Incidentally, do try to remember *not* to hit the committee boat at the end of the race.) But whereas your protest flag will be very much in evidence, your racing number is something you might do better to conceal – depending on your tactics.

You should also be prepared for the worst. If, for some reason, you have to pull out early with 'gear failure', you'll need to have handy a dramatically splintered mainsheet-block or a convincingly tangled forestay. Ideally, this should not be anything too big – so that you can then carry it up to the bar to show it off afterwards, whilst you tell your tale of how it felt when the spinnaker boom went.

○ PSYCHOLOGY ○

Pre-race psychology will play a big part in the Survival Racer's strategy. You should start psyching the opposition as soon as you sign on at the race office and pay your entry fee. Surprisingly, this is a tactic which many club competitors overlook – perhaps because they expect the race to be won by the same old people (usually the case). As an unknown quantity the Survival Racer can do a great deal to take the wind out of the opposition's sails before the start, getting them worried about his reputation as a 'savage luffer'.

So take your time as you wander through the dinghy park or through the marina, conspicuously carrying a sail-bag emblazoned with the insignia of the top sailmaker of the class. (Don't use the bag with the dwarf in – leave that to the strongman.)

In dinghy racing for example as you pass the boats of your nearest rivals, make a point of stopping to look their craft over, perhaps even offering a few friendly comments: 'just received my new Mylar genoa back from X-Co – had it recut for the third time'; 'Notice you haven't yet fitted a Harken muscle box on the boom outhaul – suppose you reckon the old system's more reliable.'

When you get to the perfectly prepared boat of the class leader, try rubbing your hand along its gleaming bottom; 'Not bad at all – I suppose you'll have it *really* smooth for the championship.'

Above all, try to appear unhurried. None of that last-minute panic. Continue your inspections, wandering around with your centreboard and rudder, occasionally polishing them with a cloth. Stroll on to the harbour wall with an anemometer, and be seen noting down wind speeds.

This does require, of course, getting your boat rigged as completely as possible the night before, then keeping everything well hidden under the cover. Thus, you and your crew (if you have one) will be able to amble past the throng at the last minute, life-jackets and wetsuits draped casually over the arm, while the others are buzzing around preparing to launch. This is basically, of course, the old 'Drake Tactic' (Bowls, 1558, Plymouth Hoe): 'Just finishing off my pint with young Jim here. Don't know what all the rush is about. There's still twenty minutes till the start.'

If, in addition, the Survival Racer (through his manoeuvrings on various club committees) has secured pole position for launching from the dinghy park and can thus be first out, he should start the race way ahead in the psychological stakes. The opposition will be left in no doubt that they're up against someone who means business.

However, the Survival Racer won't always want to put the wind up his opponents in this way. He may prefer to start as an outsider and then to come from behind. In this case, he'll avoid getting the opposition over-worried. As he walks past the other boats his remarks will be more along the lines of: 'Had to drive through the night to get here. Can't say I feel very much like racing'; 'Was up till 3 o'clock last night and that was quite a mixture we were putting away. Last time I raced after a night like that, we went half a mile wide of the weather mark'.

Your crew, of course, should appear similarly befuddled, staggering around the boat looking as if he's slept in his clothes, still trying desperately to sort things out as the ten minute gun goes.

○ **THE START** ○

Clearly, your tactics at the start will depend very much on the type of race you've selected and the sort of boat you're sailing. In an aggressive high class go-for-it race, you'll be jockeying for position with the rest of them, and keeping a close eye on the hotshots. In between false starts you'll be ploughing up and down the line in a cloud of spray, making it clear that when the gun goes and the flags are up, you'll be the one to get 'clean air' in those vital early minutes. (Be wary, of course, of getting too good a flying start if your crew still haven't woken up properly – you may lose them overboard.)

If it is a bunched start in a handicap race, you should be very well placed sailing the old fishing-smack – the others will be very wary of crowding 'Rammer' in to leeward and will tend to make way for her.

At other times, though, you'll prefer to hang back – as, for instance, when you're putting Plan 1 into operation (see below).

○ **PLAN 1** ○

Careful race selection is the key to success here. Look for the sort of course where you can take full advantage of the local geography and can capitalise on your talent for sailing an *imaginative* course.

What you need is a race taking place off a deeply indented coastline with plenty of bays and headlands. It also helps if the racing marks are out of sight of each other (none of that Olympic triangle nonsense). The ideal course would be straight out to sea from the starting line in a bay, and then back into the next bay past a convenient headland.

If the Survival Racer can make good use of that headland, the race is as good as won – though it won't seem like it as you all get ready for the off. Not for you the standard race tactic of being right on the line, at the favoured end, at full speed, bang on the gun. (Quite apart from anything else this should help you to conceal that you haven't much idea what racing is all about and that you are not exactly in full control of your sleek racing machine.)

You can even heave-to and let your sails flap, thus living up to the 'Joe Cool' image you established before the race. Try quietly smoking a cigarette, and standing up contemplating the sky – being careful not to fall in.

In fact, your aim will be to start *last* with a great deal of commotion aboard – sails flapping, sheets flying, crew cursing. The purpose of all this pantomine is to catch the attention of the race committee. They need to be given the impression that the Survival Racer (who was among the favourites) has had some serious gear failure before the start. Clearly, however, he is determined to go on against the odds. ('Just like him. Good old John. Never say die', 'What rotten luck' etc.) These facts, of course, will be confirmed (by you) afterwards: 'Main halyard went at the five-minute gun – held it in my teeth, but took a while to splice it back in that wind!'

Once he does get under way, the Survival Racer moves quickly to put into effect the first part of his pre-planned strategy. Instead of sailing out to the first mark, he will find himself veering towards that headland. Once out of sight of the committee boat, he will capsize by a handy beach on the headland – preferably at a spot close to some good tree cover.

There he will be met by his wife or other trusted hanger-on concealed amid the trees with the car and the launching trolley. They will then be able to haul the boat across the headland and relaunch on the other side. From here the Survival Sailor should easily be able to slip back on to the more orthodox race course – *several miles ahead of the rest of the fleet.* (cf. Xerxes, hauling his ships across the Isthmus of Actium, shortly before the Battle of Salamis in 480 BC.)

He can then gingerly sail the rest of the course, taking his time and allowing the club champion to almost catch him on the line. Throughout the race the Survival Racer's sails probably will be incompetently trimmed but the original gear failure story will account for this.

Once the race is won, the Survival Racer should show his usual generosity of spirit – particularly towards the club champion: 'You gave me a real old run for my money, Martin. Thought you were going to make it at one point.' And as friends and admirers crowd round to congratulate the Survival Racer at the bar: 'Drinks on me, chaps. Actually it was young Jim who did it for me.' (He was the one who pulled the boat across the headland.)

○ PLAN 2 ○

Here you'll be going for a boat-to-boat race in the old fishing smack or converted lifeboat. If you've taken the trouble to carefully select a handicap competition which is raced around a short course with a large number of laps, you should have ample opportunity to cripple the other boats as they come past you. (Many of them will probably complete two laps to every one of yours – but this shouldn't matter too much with your very high handicap.)

This is the sort of race where your crew really will have to work together as a team: your hailer and your strongman should be able to ensure that only about a quarter of the entrants actually finish the race; and your midget will need to have his eyes everywhere to spot the leaders of each class so that you can concentrate on putting *these* boats out of action; the commodore's niece will come into her own *after* the race, since there are almost bound to be a large number of appeals to the protest committee, seeking to deny you your well-earned victory.

One tip: don't leave yourself with everything to do during the race itself. You should be able to hole a number of other boats on the starting line by discreetly engineered collisions. Grasp all the opportunities that come your way on the starting line; thus, when asked by other competitors what course number has been selected (you are blocking their view of the committee boat), take the chance to give the *wrong* number. You can even get to work before casting off and heading out: early that morning take the opportunity to remove the drain plugs from some of your competitor's boats, replacing them with a soft wax which will dissolve in the course of the race. This could easily take care of half a dozen of the fastest members of the fleet.

○ PLAN 3 ○

This will work best in conditions of poor visibility, and is almost foolproof in thick fog. You should be in a 'go-faster' boat that looks as if it *might* be capable of winning – if properly handled. The idea is to pick a two-lap (or ideally three-lap) course, *which you then will proceed to sail very, very wide,* keeping out of view of the rest of the fleet. There's no harm in making your intentions clear right from the start, i.e. if all the leaders are going to the port side of the course, go the other way. (You may even find that they make the wrong decision – thus adding to your reputation – though this doesn't happen all that often.)

Your tactic will be to take your time, and only to complete *one* lap, steering clear of the other competitors, and then sailing jubilantly across the finish line, with the rest of the fleet now bearing down on you and having been round three times. It's vital, if using this tactic, to have another boat ready to testify that you *did* in fact go round *three* times. (As already mentioned, this is something you will have to set up in advance.)

○ PLAN 4 ○

Only to be used as a last resort, if for some reason one of your other more 'orthodox' race plans doesn't look like panning out. You may, for instance, find yourself left on the line with sails flapping, having great difficulty in getting under way at all, and with the fleet fast disappearing up the windward leg.

Provided, however, you are on an Olympic-type triangular course which has to be rounded at least twice, you can still save the situation. Just sail slowly up the first windward leg – once you manage to get going; and on arrival at the mark (making sure there are no stragglers around to see), take out a pair of shears and get the strongman to cut the cable releasing the buoy to drift away.

You then sail on a bit from the scene of the crime, before capsizing and returning to the club with the usual gear failure story. When the fleet comes to round the windward mark – for the second time – it will be only to find there isn't one – and the committee, with any luck, will cancel the race.

○ THE POST MORTEM ○

Of course, there is always a risk that even if you give your all and carry out one of the Survival Racing plans to perfection, you may still be pipped at the post. In these cases, it's no good crying over spilt milk. After all, you've done your best. But it may be helpful to have a few excuses handy: you might perhaps have stopped to rescue someone in distress (never mind that it was you who got them into distress in the first place); gear failure ('clapped out sails', 'weeds on the rudder fittings') is another good standby. But sabotage is often even better – and, again, make sure you bring the evidence to the bar with you so that everyone can see the frayed trapeze wire that some blackguard obviously spent last night sawing away at.

If you're skipper, of course, you can always blame it on your crew ('Just one bad tack after another'.) But if you're crew, you'll probably take a different view ('If the skipper had tacked when I told him, we'd have stayed ahead and won easily'). The owner, you can be sure, will also bear his share of the responsibility ('Why does he always want to take over the steering at those crucial moments . . . ').

Then, of course, there's always the wind – *they* caught all the shifts; or dirty tricks by one of the other boats; or the race committee's incompetence at setting the course; or the race officer's insane decision to go for a downwind start, or indeed sheer bad luck.

But let's not anticipate the worst. With any luck, none of these explanations will prove to be necessary. If you've managed to pull it off, *you* will be the one listening to everyone else at the bar make excuses. And excuses, make no mistake, as you'll tell your team-mates, is what they are: 'That was no "flukey wind" as the others are claiming – it was the sort of shifting wind that really sorts out who can sail and who can't.'

However, in the event that victory does come your way – much as you deserved it – it may be advisable not to push your luck too far. This is the moment when the Survival Racer might do well to recall the advice given at the beginning of this chapter – especially now that you have some laurels to rest on: when it comes to racing – *don't*.

○ RACING

Whenever you get a perfect start, the race will be recalled

On the beat, if *you* tack on the shifts, it will not pay

It will for everyone else

What seemed to be the layline when you tacked will turn out not to have been the layline when you reach the mark

When you are in the lead, the wind will strengthen from behind

When you're behind, the wind will strengthen up ahead

If one boat hoists a spinnaker, they all will

Whenever you are in the lead on the final leg, either

        a) the wind will drop, or
        b) the time limit will expire, or
        c) you will hit the committee boat

SAM LLEWELLYN

DEAD RECKONING

Picturesque Pulteney, a charming fishing village and a yachting haven for the wealthy on the south coast, is home to whizz-kid boat designer Charlie Agutter. But beneath the gleaming hulls lurks deadly treachery. For someone is out to get Charlie. Someone who doesn't care who else gets hurt in the process. Charlie's brother is dead – and everyone is blaming Charlie, designer of the revolutionary new yacht that killed him. Charlie knew it had to be sabotage.

It looks like a personal vendetta. But with the Captain's Cup approaching fast, and serious money at stake, something more sinister is bringing the surf to the boil. Charlie will have to move swiftly if he is going to save his career and still win the race . . .

'The Dick Francis of ocean racing' *Sunday Express*

0 7474 0086 5   ADVENTURE THRILLER   £2.99

A THOROUGHLY LEWD COLLECTION OF EXCEEDINGLY RUDE RHYMES!!

Ribald, ingenious, hilariously blue – this side-splitting selection of bawdy limericks will have you reeling with riotous laughter and mirth-filled merriment. There's Adam complacently stroking his madam . . . Irene who made an offering quite obscene . . . Hyde who fell down a privy and died . . . the young fellow of Kent who had a peculiar bent . . . the brainy professor named Zed who dreamed of a buxom co-ed . . . and many, many more!

0 7221 1297 1   HUMOUR £1.95

THE MENSA PUZZLE·BOOK

PHILIP CARTER & KEN RUSSELL

This challenging collection of Mensa puzzles is not for the faint-hearted. You'll need all your wits about you to solve the dazzling range of brainteasers – crosswords, word and number games, grid and diagram puzzles – a veritable cornucopia of craftiness.

THE ULTIMATE QUIZ BOOK FOR THE ULTIMATE QUIZ ADDICT

0 7474 0018 7   CROSSWORDS/QUIZZES   £2.99

A selection of bestsellers from SPHERE

FICTION

JUBILEE: THE POPPY CHRONICLES 1	Claire Rayner	£3.50 ☐
DAUGHTERS	Suzanne Goodwin	£3.50 ☐
REDCOAT	Bernard Cornwell	£3.50 ☐
WHEN DREAMS COME TRUE	Emma Blair	£3.50 ☐
THE LEGACY OF HEOROT	Niven/Pournelle/Barnes	£3.50 ☐

FILM AND TV TIE-IN

BUSTER	Colin Shindler	£2.99 ☐
COMING TOGETHER	Alexandra Hine	£2.99 ☐
RUN FOR YOUR LIFE	Stuart Collins	£2.99 ☐
BLACK FOREST CLINIC	Peter Heim	£2.99 ☐
INTIMATE CONTACT	Jacqueline Osborne	£2.50 ☐

NON-FICTION

BARE-FACED MESSIAH	Russell Miller	£3.99 ☐
THE COCHIN CONNECTION	Alison and Brian Milgate	£3.50 ☐
HOWARD & MASCHLER ON FOOD	Elizabeth Jane Howard and Fay Maschler	£3.99 ☐
FISH	Robyn Wilson	£2.50 ☐
THE SACRED VIRGIN AND THE HOLY WHORE	Anthony Harris	£3.50 ☐

All Sphere books are available at your local bookshop or newsagent, or can be ordered direct from the publisher. Just tick the titles you want and fill in the form below.

Name _____

Address _____

_____

Write to Sphere Books, Cash Sales Department, P.O. Box 11, Falmouth, Cornwall TR10 9EN

Please enclose a cheque or postal order to the value of the cover price plus:

UK: 60p for the first book, 25p for the second book and 15p for each additional book ordered to a maximum charge of £1.90.

OVERSEAS & EIRE: £1.25 for the first book, 75p for the second book and 28p for each subsequent title ordered.

BFPO: 60p for the first book, 25p for the second book plus 15p per copy for the next 7 books, thereafter 9p per book.

Sphere Books reserve the right to show new retail prices on covers which may differ from those previously advertised in the text elsewhere, and to increase postal rates in accordance with the P.O.